STUDY GUIDE FOR

THE CODES GUIDEBOOK
FOR INTERIORS

Third Edition

Mary Hue

STUDY GUIDE FOR

THE CODES GUIDEBOOK FOR INTERIORS

Third Edition

Sharon Koomen Harmon, IIDA
Katherine E. Kennon, AIA

WILEY

John Wiley & Sons, Inc.

For general information on our other products and services or for technical support, please contact our Customer Care Department within the United States at 800-762-2974, outside the United States at (317) 572-3993 or fax (317) 572-4002.

Wiley also publishes its books in a variety of electronic formats. Some content that appears in print may not be available in electronic books. For more information about Wiley products, visit our web site at www.wiley.com.

Library of Congress Cataloging-in-Publication Data:

Harmon, Sharon Koomen, 1964–

Study guide for the codes guidebook for interiors / Sharon Koomen Harmon, Katherine E. Kennon—3rd ed.

   p. cm.

ISBN 0-471-65089-7 (pbk.)

1. Interior decorators—United States—Handbooks, manuals, etc. 2. Building laws—United States. I. Title: Codes guidebook for interiors. II. Kennon, Katherine E. III. Title.

KF5701.Z9H37 2005

343.73'078624—dc22

                                  2004017037

Printed in the United States of America

10 9 8 7 6 5 4 3 2 1

CONTENTS

INTRODUCTION: ABOUT THIS BOOK   ix

SECTION 1   **KEY TERMS BY CHAPTER**   1

SECTION 2   **SHORT-ANSWER QUESTIONS**   9

Chapter 1   *About the Codes / 9*
Chapter 2   *Occupancy Classifications and Loads / 11*
Chapter 3   *Construction Types and Building Sizes / 14*
Chapter 4   *Means of Egress / 16*
Chapter 5   *Fire-Resistant Materials and Assemblies / 20*
Chapter 6   *Fire Protection Systems / 23*
Chapter 7   *Plumbing and Mechanical Requirements / 26*
Chapter 8   *Electrical and Communication Requirements / 30*
Chapter 9   *Finish and Furniture Selection / 34*
Chapter 10   *Code Officials and the Code Process / 38*

SECTION 3   **STUDY PROBLEMS**   41

Chapter 1   *About the Codes / 41*
Chapter 2   *Occupancy Classifications and Loads / 43*
Chapter 3   *Construction Types and Building Sizes / 49*
Chapter 4   *Means of Egress / 51*
Chapter 5   *Fire-Resistant Materials and Assemblies / 58*
Chapter 6   *Fire Protection Systems / 61*
Chapter 7   *Plumbing and Mechanical Requirements / 62*
Chapter 8   *Electrical and Communication Requirements / 64*
Chapter 9   *Finish and Furniture Selection / 64*
Chapter 10   *Code Officials and the Code Process / 68*

SECTION 4   **ANSWERS TO SHORT-ANSWER QUESTIONS**   69

SECTION 5   **ANSWERS TO STUDY PROBLEMS**   83

APPENDIX A   **CODE TABLES**   105

APPENDIX B   **FULL-SIZE CHECKLISTS**   119

ACKNOWLEDGMENTS

Thank you to everyone who helped make this book possible. Thank you to Amanda Miller, Vice President and Publisher at John Wiley & Sons, Inc., for the continued support, as well as Paul Drougas, Acquisitions Editor, and Shannon Egan, Production Editor, for their combined efforts.

INTRODUCTION
ABOUT THIS BOOK

This third edition *Study Guide* has been updated to complement the new edition of *The Codes Guidebook for Interiors*. It is designed as a study tool. It can be used in the classroom as homework or for test problems, in conjunction with studio design projects, by an individual as a self-study tool, and by designers when preparing for the NCIDQ and other licensing exams.

The *Study Guide* has been divided into five sections. Each section has been organized to parallel the ten chapters in *The Codes Guidebook for Interiors* so that you can read a chapter in the book and then answer the corresponding questions in the *Study Guide*. **Section 1** of the *Study Guide* lists the key terms found in each chapter, giving you a general awareness of the topics in each chapter of the *Guidebook*. This section also provides you with a starting point for studying, allowing you to define and study the terms as you wish.

Section 2 concentrates on short-answer questions. These include True/False, fill-in-the-blank, and multiple-choice questions. The answers to these questions can be found within the text of the corresponding chapter in the *Guidebook*. The questions have been developed specifically to test the retention of the material within each chapter and to review the basic concepts presented within the text. (The notes found in the margins of the *Guidebook* were not used in developing these questions.)

Section 3 of the *Study Guide* consists of study problems. Although some of the study problems are very direct and require memorization, most of them have been developed so that you can apply what you have learned to realistic design situations. Similar to the many examples provided in the *Guidebook*, a variety of design scenarios are used. Some of them test your ability to use the various code tables in the *Guidebook*. Other problems may require a code calculation or specific knowledge of a standard.

Section 4 provides you with the answers to the short answer questions in Section 2. This section is invaluable because it provides you not only with the answers, but also with an explanation of each answer. The answers to the study problems in Section 3 can be found in **Section 5**. They provide you with a comprehensive, step-by-step explanation of how the answers are obtained, including how to read each code table and how each calculation is determined.

The last part of the *Study Guide* consists of two appendices. **Appendix A** provides you with the code tables you are asked to reference when doing the study problems. They have been reprinted from the *Guidebook* for your convenience. In **Appendix B**, you will find all the checklists used in the *Guidebook*. They have been reprinted in standard size so they will be easier to use. Feel free to copy and use them in your design projects.

As you work through this *Study Guide*, you will gain confidence in your knowledge of codes, standards, and federal regulations, and you will learn how to apply the codes to real interior projects.

SECTION 1

KEY TERMS BY CHAPTER

CHAPTER 1. About the Codes

Access Board

Accessible

Americans with Disabilities Act (ADA)

Americans with Disabilities Act Accessibility Guidelines (ADAAG)

American National Standards Institute (ANSI)

American Society of Heating, Refrigeration, and Air Conditioning Engineers (ASHRAE)

American Society for Testing and Materials (ASTM)

Architectural Barriers Act (ABA)

Architectural and Transportation Barriers Compliance Board (ATBCB)

Building Officials and Code Administrators International (BOCA)

Code

Code of Federal Regulations (CFR)

Commercial facility

Common Code Format

Department of Housing and Urban Development (HUD)

Department of Justice (DOJ)

Fair Housing Act (FHA)

Federal Register (FR)

Federal regulation

ICC Electrical Code—Administrative Provisions (ICCEC)

ICC Performance Code for Buildings and Facilities (ICCPC)

International Building Code (IBC)

International Code Council (ICC)

International Conference of Building Officials (ICBO)

International Energy Conservation Code (IECC)

International Existing Building Code (IEBC)

International Fire Code (IFC)

International Mechanical Code (IMC)

International Plumbing Code (IPC)

International Residential Code (IRC)

Legacy code

Life Safety Code (LSC or NFPA 101)

Manual of Style

National Electrical Code (NEC or NFPA 70)

National Fire Protection Association (NFPA)

NFPA 900 Building Energy Code (NFPA 900)

NFPA 5000 Building Construction and Safety Code (NFPA 5000)

One and Two Family Dwelling Code (OTFDC)

Performance code

Prescriptive code

Public accommodation

Southern Building Code Congress International (SBCCI)

Standard

Underwriters Laboratories (UL)

Uniform Fire Code (UFC or NFPA 1)

Uniform Mechanical Code (UMC)

Uniform Plumbing Code (UPC)

Uniform Federal Accessibility Standards (UFAS)

CHAPTER 2. Occupancy Classifications and Loads

Accessory occupancy

Actual number

Ancillary space

Assembly occupancy

Building type (or use)

Business occupancy

Calculated number

Detentional/Correctional occupancy

Dwelling unit

Educational occupancy

Factory occupancy

Fixed seating
Floor area
Fuel load
Gross square feet
Habitable space or room
Hazard
Hazardous occupancy
Health Care occupancy
Incidental use area or room
Increased number
Industrial occupancy
Institutional occupancy
Living area or room
Load factor
Mercantile occupancy
Miscellaneous occupancy
Mixed multiple occupancy
Multiple uses
Net square feet
Non-separated mixed occupancy
Occupancy classification
Occupancy subclassification
Occupant
Occupant load
Occupiable space or room
Primary space (or use)
Residential occupancy
Restrained
Risk factor
Separated mixed occupancy
Separated multiple occupancy
Sleeping area or room
Storage occupancy
Subclassification
Transient lodging
Unrestrained
Unusual use or occupancy
Unusual structure
Use group
Utility occupancy

CHAPTER 3. Construction Types and Building Sizes

Atrium
Basement

Building area
Building element
Building height
Combustible
Construction type
Fire-resistant rating
Fire resistive
Fire retardant
Fire wall
Floor area
Heavy timber
High-rise building
Limited combustible
Mezzanine
Noncombustible
Party wall
Protected
Story height
Structural element
Unprotected

CHAPTER 4. Means of Egress

Accessible hardware
Aisle
Aisle accessway
Alcove
Area of refuge
Clearance
Common path of travel
Corridor
Dead-end corridor
Discharge corridor
Door
Door swing
Egress court
Elevator
Emergency lighting
Escalator
Exit
Exit access
Exit discharge
Exit passageway
Exit sign
Exit stair
Exit width

Exterior exit door
Foyer
Freight elevator
Guard
Half diagonal rule
Handrail
Horizontal exit
Horizontal run
Intervening room
Landing
Level variable
Main lobby
Means of egress
Moving walk
Multi-story
Natural path of travel
Nosing
Occupant load
Passageway
Passenger elevator
Public way
Ramp
Riser
Stair variable
Stairway
Story
Tenant
Travel distance
Tread
Turning space (or circle)
Unobstructed path
Vertical rise
Vestibule

CHAPTER 5. Fire-Resistant Materials and Assemblies

Active fire-protection system
Automatic closing
Ceiling damper
Clear ceramic
Compartmentation
Construction assembly
Corridor wall
Damper system
Demising wall

Draftstop
Evacuation
Fire area
Fire barrier
Fire blocking
Fire damper
Fire door assembly
Fire exit hardware
Fire load
Fire partition
Fire-protection rating
Fire-rated assembly
Fire rating
Fire-resistance rating
Fire resistant
Fire separation wall
Firestop
Fire wall
Fire window assembly
Floor/ceiling assembly
Fuel load
F-rating
Glass block
Horizontal exit
Incidental use area or room
Labeled assembly
Laminated glass
Membrane penetration
Occupancy separation
Opening protective
Panic hardware
Party wall
Passive fire-protection system
Pressurization system
Rated glazing
Roof/ceiling assembly
Room separation
Self-closing
Smoke barrier
Smoke compartment
Smoke damper
Smoke partition
Smokestop door assembly
Tenant separation
Test ratings

Through-penetration
Through-penetration protective
Transparent wall unit
T-rating
Ventilation system
Vertical shaft enclosure
Vestibule
Wall assembly
Window assembly
Wire glass

CHAPTER 6. Fire Protection Systems

Accessible warning system
Alarm notification appliance
Alarm system
Alternate extinguishing system
Audible alarm
Audio system
Automatic fire extinguishing system
Automatic sprinkler system
Carbon monoxide detector
Deluge system
Detection system
Dry pipe system
Emergency alarm system
Extended coverage sprinkler head
Extinguishing system
Fast-response sprinkler head
Fire area
Fire detector
Fire extinguisher
Fire hose
Fire protection system
Flashover
Fusible link
Heat detector
Initiating device
Integrated alarm
Large drop sprinkler head
Manual fire alarm
Multiple station
Open head sprinkler
Preaction system
Prevention system

Quick-response sprinkler head
Radiant heat
Residential sprinkler head
Single station
Smoke detector
Sprinkler head
Standard spray sprinkler head
Standpipe
Suppression system
Visual alarm
Voice communication system
Wet pipe system
Zone

CHAPTER 7. Plumbing and Mechanical Requirements

Access panel
Accessible fixture
Accessory
Air circulation
Ambulatory accessible stall
Bathing room or facility
Bathroom
Bathtub
Clearance
Clear floor space
Clothes washer
Conditioned air
Cooling load
Customer toilet facility
Damper
Dishwasher
Drinking fountain
Duct
Employee/customer toilet facility
Energy efficient
Exhaust air
Family toilet facility
Front approach
Grab bar
International Mechanical Code (IMC)
International Plumbing Code (IPC)
Kitchen sink
Kneespace
Lavatory

Licensed contractor
Load factor
Mechanical room
Multiple-bathing facility
Multiple-toilet facility
Occupant load
Plenum
Plumbing fixture
Potty parity
Private toilet facility
Reach ranges
Restroom
Return air
Shower
Side approach
Signage
Single-bathing facility
Single-toilet facility
Sink
Soil pipe
Supply air
Thermostat
Toespace
Toilet room or facility
Toilet stall
Turning space (or circle)
Uniform Mechanical Code (UMC)
Uniform Plumbing Code (UPC)
Unisex facility
Urinal
Utility sink
Ventilation
Ventilation air
Waste pipe
Water closet
Water conservation
Wheelchair accessible stall
Zone

CHAPTER 8. Electrical and Communication Requirements

Alarm system
Appliance
Arc fault circuit interrupter (AFCI)
Assistive listening system
Audio systems

Backup power source
Bandwidth
Branch panelboard
Building telephone system
Cable
Cable service
Circuit
Circuit breaker
Circuit interrupter
Coaxial cable
Communication room
Communication system
Composite cable
Computer system
Concealed
Conductor
Conduit
Dedicated circuit
Dedicated outlet
Device
Electrical box
Electrical panel
Emergency electrical system
Energy efficient
Equipment
Fail Safe
Fail Secure
Fiber optic cable
Flat wire
Flex (or BX) cable
Fuse
Ground fault circuit interrupter (GFCI or GFl)
Grounding
ICC Electrical Code (ICCEC)
Intercom system
International Energy Conservation Code (IECC)
Junction box
Labeled fixture or device
Light fixture
Low voltage cable
Metal clad cable
National Electrical Code (NEC)
Outlet
Outlet box
Panelboard

Public telephone
Raceway
Receptacle outlet
Romex cable
Satellite closet
Satellite system
Security system
Standby power system
Surveillance system
Switch
Switchboard
Switch box
Switching room
Telecommunication room
Telecommunication system
Telephone
Telephone bank
Telephone closet
Television system
Twisted pair cable
Uninterrupted power supply system
Video systems
Voice communication system
Voice/data outlet
Voltage
Wireless

CHAPTER 9. Finish and Furniture Selection

Back coating
California Technical Bulletin #133 (CAL 133 or TB 133)
Ceiling finish
Ceiling treatment
Certificate of Flame Resistance
Char mark
Cigarette Ignition Test
Clear knee space
Component
Critical radiant flux
Decorative materials
Decorative vegetation
Detectable warning
Expanded vinyl wallcovering
Fabric
Finish

Finish class
Finish rating
Fire block
Fire retardant
Flame resistant
Flame source
Flame spread index (FSI)
Flammability
Flashover
Floor covering
Floor finish
Foam (or cellular) plastic
Fuel load
Full-scale test
Furnishing finish
Furniture
Furring strip
Heat barrier
Ignition source
Interior finish
Large-scale test
LEED
Light transmitting plastic
Mattress Test
Mock-up
Movable partition
Nontested finish
Pass/fail test
Pill Test
Pitts Test
Plastic
Pretested finish
Radiant heat
Radiant Panel Test
Ranked test
Rated test
Room Corner Test
Safety glass
Seating
Small-scale test
Smoke Density Test
Smoke development index (SDI)
Smolder
Smolder Resistance Test
Steiner Tunnel Test

Sustainability
Testing company
Toxicity Test
Treated
Treatment company
Trim
Upholstered seating
Upholstered Seating Test
Upholstery
Vertical Flame Test
Vertical treatment
Wallcovering
Wall finish
Wall hanging
Window treatment
Worksurface

CHAPTER 10. Code Officials and the Code Process

Acceptable methods
Alternate methods
Appeal
Approved
Authority Having Jurisdiction (AHJ)
Board of Appeals
Building inspector
Certificate of Completion (C of C)
Certificate of Occupancy (C of O)
Certified Building Official (CBO)
Code department
Code official
Code publication
Code research
Compliance

Computer modeling
Construction documents
Construction drawing(s)
Documentation
Engineering calculation(s)
Equivalency
Final inspection
Final review
Fire marshal
Floor plan(s)
Health code
Inspection
Interior project
Jurisdiction
Liability
Licensed contractor
Local agency
Ordinance
Performance design
Performance documentation
Permit
Phased Certificate of Occupancy
Plan review
Plans examiner
Preliminary review
Record (as-built) drawing(s)
Specification(s)
Subcontractor
Temporary Certificate of Occupancy
Use and occupancy letter
Variance
Walk-through

SECTION 2

SHORT-ANSWER QUESTIONS

☐ CHAPTER 1. About the Codes

1. Federal buildings, such as VA hospitals and military office buildings, are usually not subject to state and local building codes.   True/False

2. Typically, no two code jurisdictions have exactly the same codes and standards requirements.   True/False

3. Many states have developed a custom building code using the *International Building Code* as the model.   True/False

4. The NFPA *National Electrical Code* is the most widely used electrical code.   True/False

5. ADA is an accessibility code for the design of public buildings.   True/False

6. Standards have no legal standing on their own.   True/False

7. Codes and standards set only minimum criteria; when designing a project, stricter requirements can be followed.   True/False

8. If it is decided that performance codes will be used on a project, the entire project must be designed using performance codes.   True/False

9. The *Life Safety Code* is organized by the Common Code Format.   True/False

10. What does *ADAAG* stand for? _____

11. The *Life Safety Code* is different from the *International Building Code* because it organizes most of its chapters by_____.

12. What is another name for the Architectural and Transportation Barriers Compliance Board?
_____

13. Name two states or cities that use a customized code: _____

14. Which standards organization is recognized worldwide for its logo, which is attached to all products it approves? _____

15. Which of the following groups of codes is published as separate documents by the International Code Council, but not by the NFPA?
    a. Residential code, energy code, and electrical code
    b. Energy code, performance code, and residential code
    c. Performance code, residential code, and existing building code
    d. Existing building code, electrical code, and performance code

16. Which of the following is not a typical part of using performance codes?
    a. Working with a code official starts in the early stages of the project.
    b. An overall team approach should be taken with the client as the team leader.
    c. Supporting documentation should be provided to support your unique design.
    d. A number of parameters or risk factors should be determined at the beginning of the project.

17. You should use a fire code in conjunction with a building code on a project when:
    a. It is required by the jurisdiction.
    b. You are designing for an occupancy that is considered more hazardous.
    c. You are working on a building that requires an emergency planning system.
    d. a and b only
    e. All of the above

18. Which of the following does the ADA regulate?
    a. Public transportation
    b. Telecommunication services
    c. Commercial facilities
    d. Federal office buildings
    e. a, b, and c
    f. b and c only

19. What is the difference between ADA and *ADAAG*?
    a. One is an organization and the other is a publication.
    b. One is the law and the other is a publication.
    c. They are the same thing.
    d. They do not have anything to do with each other.

20. Which of the following is *not* a federal regulation?
    a. Americans with Disabilities Act
    b. Architectural Barriers Act
    c. Fair Housing Act
    d. American Standards Act
    e. All of the above are federal regulations.

21. Which standards organization approves the standards developed by others rather than concentrating on developing its own?
    a. ANSI
    b. UL
    c. ASHRAE
    d. ASTM

22. Which of the following does *not* address accessibility issues?
    a. *UFAS*
    b. ADA
    c. ICC/ANSI
    d. *ADAAG*
    e. All of the above address accessibility issues.

23. What do you do if you are required to use two different code publications for a project and there is a conflicting code requirement?
    a. Use the requirement found in the most recent code publication.
    b. Compare the two requirements and use the most restrictive one.
    c. Pick one or the other as long as it is required by one of the publications.
    d. None of the above

24. To determine which codes are required in a jurisdiction, who should you ask?
    a. The code official in the jurisdiction of your office
    b. The code official in the jurisdiction of your project
    c. The client of your project
    d. The licensed contractor working on your project

CHAPTER 2. Occupancy Classifications and Loads

1. Determining the occupancy classification(s) of a project should be one of the first steps in researching codes.   **True/False**

2. If there are two occupancies in the same building and one is smaller than the other, the smaller occupancy is known as an accessory occupancy.   **True/False**

3. Instead of being considered a separate storage occupancy, small storage rooms are always treated as part of the predominating occupancy.   **True/False**

4. Locations of fire-resistance-rated walls are important in buildings with more than one occupancy classifications.   **True/False**

5. The NFPA codes such as the *Life Safety Code* subdivide Institutional occupancies into several different categories. Name two of them: _____ _____

6. The various types of hazardous situations that can occur in a building are also often referred to as _____ by the codes. _____

7. When measuring a building to determine the occupant load, _____ square feet (square meters) refers to the building area that includes all miscellaneous (or ancillary) spaces.

8. The codes divide the type of hazardous occupancies into four main categories: fire, explosive, _____, and _____ .

9. Using the *International Building Code* classifications, match each building type on the left with its typical occupancy classification shown on the right. Fill in the appropriate letter on the lines shown.

   ___ Supermarket   a. Institutional occupancy
   ___ Refinery   b. Hazardous occupancy
   ___ Gas plant   c. Business occupancy
   ___ Bank   d. Assembly occupancy
   ___ Nursing home   e. Storage occupancy
   ___ Kindergarten   f. Mercantile occupancy
   ___ Dormitory   g. Industrial occupancy
   ___ Church   h. Educational occupancy
   ___ Freight terminal   i. Residential occupancy

10. Which three items help to determine the occupancy classification or subclassification of a project?
    a. Type of hazards, type of activity occurring, and size of building
    b. Size of the building, type of wall ratings, and type of activity occurring
    c. Type of activity occurring, type of hazards, and number of occupants
    d. Size of the building, number of occupants, and type of wall ratings

11. The *Life Safety Code* distinguishes between new and existing occupancies. Which of the following scenarios would typically *not* create a new occupancy?
    a. A company that is reducing the size of its tenant space
    b. A company that is hiring a number of new employees
    c. A company that is relocating to another building
    d. A company that is moving into its new office headquarters
    e. None of the above would create a new occupancy.

12. In the *International Building Code*, which of the following occupancy classifications is affected by the number of occupants?
    a. Assembly and Institutional
    b. Educational and Residential
    c. Assembly and Educational
    d. Residential and Institutional

13. Which of the following use types is usually *not* considered an Educational occupancy?
    a. College classrooms
    b. High school classrooms
    c. Elementary school classrooms
    d. Nursery school classrooms

14. Which of the following building types may *not* always be considered a Residential occupancy?
    a. Monasteries
    b. Half-way houses
    c. Nursing homes
    d. Hotels
    e. Condominiums

15. Which of the following building types would be the least likely to be a mixed occupancy?
    a. Restaurant
    b. High-security prison
    c. High school
    d. Hotel
    e. Mall

16. Which of the following occupancy classifications is currently *not* heavily regulated as a public accommodation by the Americans with Disabilities Act?
    a. Institutional
    b. Business
    c. Factories
    d. Mercantile

17. Which of the following statements about accessory occupancies is *not* true?
    a. When an accessory occupancy exists within a primary occupancy, most of the code requirements are based on the primary occupancy.
    b. The area of an accessory occupancy must be less than 10 percent of the primary occupancy's area.
    c. To be considered an accessory occupancy the allowable area within the construction type of a building or space must also be considered.
    d. All the above items are true.

18. When there is more than one type of occupancy in the same building, in which case must they meet the requirements of the most stringent occupancy classification?
    a. If they are considered separated mixed occupancies
    b. If they are considered non-separated mixed occupancies
    c. If they are considered mixed multiple occupancies
    d. If they are considered separated multiple occupancies
    e. b and c

19. In some cases you may decide to increase the occupant load of a space so that it is higher than that determined by the load factor. When you do so, you must also:
    a. Make sure you provide additional exiting as required for the increased number
    b. Make sure all the walls within the building or space are rated
    c. Typically get approval from code official for the increased number
    d. a and c only
    e. All of the above

20. Why is it important to determine the occupant load of a space?
    a. It is needed to determine the total required exit width for the space.
    b. It is needed to determine the maximum number of people allowed in the space.
    c. It is needed to determine the number of plumbing fixtures required for the space.
    d. a and c only
    e. All of the above

21. What do you need to know in order to determine the required occupant load for a space?
    a. Load factor and building type
    b. Building type and occupancy classification
    c. Number of occupants and load factor
    d. Load factor and square footage

22. When a building has a mixed occupancy, the occupant load for the whole building is determined by:
    a. The occupancy that allows the largest number of people
    b. The occupancy with the most square feet (square meter)
    c. The occupancy with the highest load factor
    d. By combining the requirements of each occupancy

23. If a space has multiple uses, the occupant load for that space is determined by:
    a. The use that indicates the largest concentration of people
    b. The use that occupies the space the most often
    c. The use that has the highest load factor
    d. The total occupant load for all the uses

24. When calculating occupant loads, seats are considered fixed if:
    a. The seats are not easily moved.
    b. The seats are continuous without arms.
    c. The seats are used on a more permanent basis.
    d. a and b only
    e. All of the above

□ CHAPTER 3. Construction Types and Building Sizes

1. Interior walls and partitions are required to be rated in Type I and Type II construction.   **True/False**

2. When comparing the different types of construction, Type V is considered the least restrictive and requires the lowest fire ratings.   **True/False**

3. Most combustible construction materials can be treated to gain some amount of fire resistance.   **True/False**

4. Buildings must consistently be updated to meet the construction type requirements within the newest building codes.   **True/False**

5. The distance of an adjacent building can affect the allowed size of a new building.   **True/False**

6. A fire _____ construction material means it will not be affected by flame, heat, or hot gases.

7. Load-bearing walls, columns, and shaft enclosures are often considered _____ elements by the building codes.

8. Wood that is considered fire resistant because of its large diameter is called _____.

9. Which of the following statements about construction types is *not* correct:
   a. The main difference between Type I and Type II is the required hourly ratings.
   b. Determining if an existing building is a Type I or Type II can be difficult because they often require the same types of construction materials.
   c. Combustible materials are not allowed in Type I but they are allowed in Type II.
   d. Within the same construction type, protected is stricter than unprotected.
   e. All of the above are correct.

10. Which construction type consists of exterior walls that are noncombustible but allows interior elements to consist of combustible materials?
    a. Type I
    b. Type II
    c. Type III
    d. Type IV
    e. Type V

11. Which of the following statements about building materials is *not* correct?
    a. Iron and steel will have a rapid loss of strength unless they are encased in a protective coating.
    b. Chemically treated wood is often known as flame-resistant treated wood.
    c. Noncombustible materials typically consist of brick, concrete, and steel.
    d. Limited combustible material is a term used only by the NFPA codes.
    e. All of the above are correct.

12. Which of the following statements about fire-retardant materials is *not* correct?
    a. They will not contribute to the fuel of the fire.
    b. They will prevent or retard the passage of heat, hot gases, and flames.
    c. They will delay the spread of a fire for a designated time period.
    d. They can sometimes be substituted for materials required to be noncombustible.
    e. All of the above are correct.

13. If more than one type of construction exists within a single building, each type of construction must be separated from the other by a:
    a. Parapet wall
    b. Party wall
    c. Fire wall
    d. a and b
    e. b and c

14. Which of the following occupancy classifications typically require the strictest types of construction?
    a. Assembly and Institutional occupancies
    b. Assembly and Residential occupancies
    c. Mercantile and Assembly occupancies
    d. Institutional and Residential occupancies

15. In order to determine if a certain occupancy classification can be located in a specific building, which of the following do you need to know?
    a. The construction type of the building
    b. The square footage (square meter) or area of the building
    c. If the building is sprinklered
    d. a and c only
    e. All of the above

16. A building's maximum size is limited by its:
    a. Construction type(s)
    b. Occupancy classification(s)
    c. Location
    d. a and b only
    e. All of the above

17. Which of the following would be allowed by the codes as a way of increasing the allowable area of a building?
    a. Changing the construction type from Type III to Type IV
    b. Adding more tenant separation walls
    c. Adding an automatic sprinkler system
    d. a and c
    e. All of the above

☐ CHAPTER 4. Means of Egress

1. Every path of travel throughout a building can be considered a means of egress. **True/False**

2. All doors of an exit stair must swing into the stairway. **True/False**

3. If the width of an alley or sidewalk is more than 10 feet (3048 mm) wide, it is no longer considered a public way. **True/False**

4. The main difference between a corridor and an aisle is that a corridor is typically surrounded by full-height walls and an aisle is created by furniture or equipment. **True/False**

5. No doorway can be more than 48 inches (1220 mm) wide. **True/False**

6. When determining the number of exits in a multistory building, the floor with the largest occupant load determines the number of required exits for all lower floors that lead to the ground level. **True/False**

7. The final destination in a means of egress is typically a(n) _____.

8. What are two types of door pulls that can be considered accessible? _____ and _____.

9. A stairway must have an intermediate landing if it rises more than how many feet or millimeters? _____

10. In addition to an exit sign, name another type of exiting sign that may be required by the codes: _____

11. A fire-resistance-rated corridor that connects the bottom of an exit stair to an exterior exit door is called an exit _____.

12. When three exits are required in a space, the third exit should be placed as _____ as possible.

13. Emergency lighting is also sometimes called _____ lighting.

14. Which of the following are affected by means of egress requirements?
    a. Finish selections
    b. Occupant loads
    c. Fire ratings
    d. a and c only
    e. All of the above

15. Which of the following statements about a means of egress is *not* correct?
    a. It is a continuous and unobstructed path of travel.
    b. Its final destination is always a public way.
    c. It can consist of vertical and horizontal passageways.
    d. It affects all buildings, new and existing.
    e. All of the above are correct.

16. Foyers and vestibules are examples of:
    a. Exit discharges
    b. Public ways
    c. Exit accesses
    d. Exits

17. Which of the following means of egress must always be fully enclosed?
    a. Intervening room
    b. Exit stair
    c. Exit access stair
    d. a and b
    e. All of the above

18. What is the typical head clearance required in an exit and exit accessway?
    a. 80 inches (2032 mm)
    b. 84 inches (2134 mm)
    c. 90 inches (2286 mm)
    d. 96 inches (2440 mm)

19. Which of the following is *not* considered a type of exit?
    a. Exit stair
    b. Exit corridor
    c. Area of refuge
    d. Horizontal exit

20. An accessible ramp in a means of egress should have a slope with a ratio no greater than what?
    a. 1:8
    b. 1:12
    c. 1:18
    d. 1:20

21. Which of the following statements about interior means of egress doors is *not* correct?
    a. They must always swing in the direction of exit travel.
    b. They must have a minimum clear opening of 32 inches (815 mm) wide.
    c. The floor level on both sides of the door cannot be more than ½ inch (13 mm) below the top of the threshold.
    d. They cannot reduce any required landing by more than 7 inches (118 mm) when fully open.
    e. All of the above are correct.

22. Which of the following stair-related codes is correct?
    a. The minimum riser height is 7 inches (180 mm).
    b. The minimum tread depth is 11 inches (280 mm).
    c. The maximum nosing projection is 1¼ inches (44 mm).
    d. Handrails are always required on both sides of the stairs.

23. Horizontal exits are most commonly found in which of the following occupancy classifications?
    a. Institutional occupancies
    b. Mercantile occupancies
    c. Residential occupancies
    d. Educational occupancies

24. Which of the following would most likely *not* be allowed as an intervening room as required by the means of egress codes?
    a. A reception area in an accounting firm
    b. A secretarial area in a law firm
    c. A file/supply room in an advertising firm
    d. A front lobby in a large brokerage firm

25. If an elevator is used as an exit in a means of egress, which of the following statements would *not* be correct?
    a. The elevator is required to have an area of refuge located somewhere in each floor.
    b. The elevator controls are required to be of a certain type.
    c. The elevator shaft and the adjacent lobby on each floor are required to be fire rated.
    d. The elevator is required to be connected to stand-by power.
    e. All of the above are correct.

26. Which of the following items are typically required at an area of refuge?
    a. A two-way communication device
    b. A sprinkler system
    c. A clear floor space
    d. a and c only
    e. All of the above

27. Which of the following statements is *not* correct?
    a. To calculate the exit widths for a whole building, you must calculate the occupant load for each floor separately.
    b. To calculate the exit widths for a whole floor with different occupancies, you must calculate the occupant load based on the tenant with the highest load factor.
    c. To calculate the exit widths for one room, you must calculate the occupant load for that room only.
    d. To calculate the exit widths for a corridor connecting several tenants, you must calculate the total occupant load for the floor.
    e. All of the above are correct.

28. What is the typical minimum corridor width required by the building codes in most occupancies?
    a. 32 inches (815 mm)
    b. 36 inches (914 mm)
    c. 44 inches (1118 mm)
    d. 48 inches (1220 mm)

29. In most cases, nothing is allowed to reduce the width of an exit. Which of the following is a typical exception allowed by the codes?
    a. Doors that do not project more than 7 inches (178 mm) when fully open
    b. Wall trim that is less than ½ inch (13 mm) thick
    c. Handrails that meet ADA requirements
    d. b and c
    e. All of the above

30. What is the term for the maximum distance a person should have to travel from any position in a building to the nearest exit?
   a. Means of egress
   b. Natural path of travel
   c. Common path of travel
   d. Travel distance

31. What is the maximum dead-end corridor length typically allowed by the codes in a nonsprinklered building?
   a. 15 feet (4572 mm)
   b. 20 feet (6096 mm)
   c. 25 feet (7620 mm)
   d. 30 feet (9144 mm)

32. Correctly calculating the occupant load of a space is important for determining which of the following?
   a. The number of exits
   b. The width of an exit
   c. The location of an exit
   d. a and b only
   e. All of the above

33. Which of the following statements is *not* correct?
   a. The width of an exit access corridor can typically be based on half of the required occupant load if it leads to two separate exits on the same floor.
   b. The width of an exit stairway can sometimes be reduced as it travels toward the exit discharge.
   c. One exit is often allowed in small buildings or spaces depending on the number of occupants and/or the travel distance.
   d. The total exit width required for a space can be equally distributed between the total number of exits serving the space.
   e. All of the above are correct.

34. Which of the following statements about aisle accessways at tables and chairs is *not* correct?
   a. Their required width is measured to the back of the chair, not the table.
   b. Their required width is usually less than that of the adjacent aisle.
   c. Their required width allows for 18 inches (445 mm) for a chair.
   d. Their required width may need to be increased in some cases to allow for accessibility.
   e. All of the above are correct.

CHAPTER 5. Fire-Resistant Materials and Assemblies

1. An active fire-protection system is sometimes referred to as a prevention system. True/False

2. The fire-resistance rating of a floor/ceiling assembly is controlled only by the construction type of the building. True/False

3. All fire-protected doors must have an automatic closing device. True/False

4. The fire rating of a through-penetration is typically lower than the fire rating of the construction assembly it is penetrating. True/False

5. A fire-protected door can also be used as a smokestop door. True/False

6. Fire barriers are typically used to create compartments within a building. True/False

7. Occupancy separation walls and demising walls are the same thing. True/False

8. Doors with fire-protection ratings are not allowed to have glass lites as part of the door. True/False

9. _____ walls are used to create a continuous vertical separation within a building or between two different buildings.

10. A door assembly typically consists of a door, frame, and _____.

11. A smoke barrier can consist of either a wall assembly or a full _____.

12. Match each NFPA standard on the left with the number designation shown on the right. Fill in the appropriate letter on the lines shown.

   __ Installation of Smoke Door Assemblies   a. NFPA 105
   __ Fire Doors and Fire Windows   b. NFPA 252
   __ Fire Test for Window and Glass Block Assemblies   c. NFPA 221
   __ Fire Test of Door Assemblies   d. NFPA 251
   __ Test of Fire Endurance of Building Construction and Materials   e. NFPA 80
   __ Fire Walls and Fire Barrier Walls   f. NFPA 257

13. What is the typical fire-resistance rating of a tenant separation wall?
   a. 2 hour
   b. 1½ hour
   c. 1 hour
   d. No rating is required.

14. Which of the following statements is true about firestops?
   a. They are required at through-penetrations in fire barriers.
   b. They are a means of restricting the passage of smoke, heat, and flames in concealed spaces.
   c. They can have two different ratings: a T-rating and a stricter F-rating.
   d. a and c only
   e. All of the above

15. A wall assembly with a 2-hour fire-resistance rating is typically required for which means of egress component?
    a. Exit access
    b. Public way
    c. Exit discharge
    d. Exit

16. Which of the following devices is used to prevent the movement of air, smoke, gases, and flame through large, concealed spaces?
    a. Firestops
    b. Draftstops
    c. Fireblocking
    d. Dampers

17. If a window is described as a *labeled* window, it means:
    a. It is a fire-rated window.
    b. It has a label that is permanently attached.
    c. It has been tested by a nationally recognized testing company.
    d. a and b only
    e. All of the above

18. Which of the following statements about occupancy separation is *not* correct?
    a. It is required in a mixed occupancy building, but not necessarily in a multiple occupancy building.
    b. When two different occupancies are adjacent to each other, the one requiring the higher rating applies.
    c. It may be required within a single tenant space if the space includes more than one occupancy.
    d. It includes vertical separation and horizontal separation.
    e. All of the above are correct.

19. Which of the following types of glass is typically considered to have a fire-protection rating?
    a. Wire glass
    b. Tempered glass
    c. Glass block
    d. a and c only
    e. All of the above

20. Which of the following smoke compartments require special ventilation and air circulation?
    a. Stair shafts
    b. Linen chutes
    c. Vestibules
    d. a and b only
    e. All of the above

21. Which of the following statements about fire-protected doors is correct?
    a. The quantity of hinges is regulated, but the type of hinge is not.
    b. Sills used at fire-rated doors do not typically need to meet accessibility requirements.
    c. Fire-rated doors are available as flush doors and panel doors.
    d. A variety of rated glazing can be used as lites in fire rated doors as long as they are within a certain size range.

22. Which of the following is typically considered a fire partition by the *International Building Code*?
   a. A wall between two guest rooms in a hotel.
   b. A wall between an office space and an exit access corridor.
   c. A wall between two tenants in a shopping mall.
   d. a and c only
   e. All of the above

23. Which of the following fire tests is required for safety glazing?
   a. *ASTM E152*
   b. *NFPA 252*
   c. *ANSI Z97.1*
   d. *UL 10B*

24. Which of the following can be used to help control smoke during a fire?
   a. Smoke barriers
   b. Pressurized exits
   c. Sprinklers
   d. a and b
   e. a and c

25. Which type of through-penetration is required in a duct that extends through a rated floor assembly?
   a. Draftstop
   b. Fire damper
   c. Ceiling damper
   d. None of the above

26. Which of the following statements about smoke dampers is *not* correct?
   a. Smoke dampers are typically used in ducts that penetrate smoke barriers.
   b. Smoke dampers are usually installed with a smoke detector.
   c. Smoke dampers are typically installed adjacent to a duct.
   d. Smoke dampers can be classified in one of four classes.
   e. All of the above are correct.

27. Which of the following would compromise the rating of a 1-hour fire-resistant wall assembly?
   a. Using a building material differently than specified by the manufacturer
   b. Not using rated caulk at the seams and joints
   c. Installing an electrical box in the wall cavity for a switch
   d. a and b only
   e. All of the above

28. Many of the newer types of rated glazing are not covered by the building codes. However, a jurisdiction may allow this type of glazing to be used if it passes which of the following tests?
   a. *ANSI Z97.1*
   b. *NFPA 257*
   c. *ASTM E119*
   d. *UL 10B*

CHAPTER 6. Fire Protection Systems

1. Multiple station smoke detectors are required by the codes to be tied into the building's power source, but single-station smoke detectors are not.   True/False

2. The decision to use an automatic sprinkler system, fire detection system, or smoke detection system is mostly based on budgetary concerns.   True/False

3. The codes limit the connection of fire and smoke alarm systems to the electrical system.   True/False

4. When a fire occurs, a detection system can only detect the presence of smoke.   True/False

5. An alarm can be activated both manually and automatically.   True/False

6. Manual fire alarms must typically be placed within 5 feet (1506 mm) from the latch side of an exit door.   True/False

7. Fire extinguishers must be in a glass case mounted on the wall.   True/False

8. Many alarms must now be audible and _____.

9. When required in a Class A space, the codes typically require that no occupant can be more than how many feet or millimeters from a fire extinguisher? _____

10. Match each NFPA standard on the left with the number designation shown on the right. Fill in the appropriate letter on the lines shown.

    __ Portable Fire Extinguishers   a. NFPA 70
    __ National Fire Alarm Code   b. NFPA 110
    __ National Electrical Code   c. NFPA 12
    __ Installation of Sprinkler Systems   d. NFPA 10
    __ Emergency and Standby Power Systems e. NFPA 72
    __ Fire Safety Symbols   f. NFPA 13
    __ Carbon Dioxide Extinguishing Systems g. NFPA 170

11. What type of system directs occupants out of the building during an emergency by verbal commands?
    a. Voice communication system
    b. Accessible warning system
    c. Emergency alarm system
    d. a and c
    e. All of the above

12. When specifying a visual alarm, which of the following is *not* regulated by the codes and the ADA guidelines?
    a. Height
    b. Color
    c. Intensity
    d. Flash rate and duration
    e. All of the above are regulated

13. Which of the following is *not* considered a detection system?
    a. Smoke detectors
    b. Manual fire alarms
    c. Heat detectors
    d. Firestops
    e. b and d

14. Which of the following is *not* considered an alarm system?
    a. Accessible warning system
    b. Manual fire alarm
    c. Voice communication system
    d. Emergency alarm system

15. Which of the following statements about an emergency alarm system is correct?
    a. It is required in most occupancy classifications.
    b. Its audible signal must be distinct from the fire alarm signal.
    c. It can include security, trouble, and evacuation alarms.
    d. b and c
    e. All of the above

16. Which class of standpipe is primarily designed for use by building occupants?
    a. Class I
    b. Class II
    c. Class III
    d. b and c

17. Which of the following is *not* typically used by the codes to determine if a standpipe is required in a building?
    a. The number of stories in the building
    b. The number of stairwells in the building
    c. Whether a sprinkler system is located in the building
    d. The type of occupancy located in the building

18. Which of the following would affect the need for a sprinkler system?
    a. Building size
    b. Occupancy type
    c. Specific room use
    d. a and b only
    e. All of the above

19. What type of sprinkler system would typically be used where the system would be exposed to freezing temperatures?
    a. Wet pipe system
    b. Dry pipe system
    c. Deluge system
    d. Fast response system

20. Which of the following is *not* typically allowed by the codes if an automatic sprinkler system is provided?
    a. Reclassify the occupancy type
    b. An increased travel distance
    c. A lower finish classification
    d. Lower fire resistance to some structure elements
    e. All of the above would be allowed.

21. Which of the following is *not* a type of sprinkler head?
    a. Residential
    b. Front wall
    c. Large drop
    d. Fast response

22. How much clearance is typically required below the head or deflector of a sprinkler?
    a. 12 inches (305 mm)
    b. 18 inches (455 mm)
    c. 24 inches (610 mm)
    d. 30 inches (762 mm)

23. Which of the following statements about fire-related codes is *not* correct?
    a. They focus on protecting occupants exiting a building and firefighters entering a building during a fire.
    b. They control building materials such as ducts, wiring, and pipes.
    c. They are not affected by accessibility codes.
    d. They include provisions for fire protection and smoke protection.
    e. All of the above are correct.

24. Which of the following specialty types of rooms or areas is the least likely to require a sprinkler head by the codes?
    a. Restaurant kitchen
    b. Atrium
    c. Trash chute
    d. Boiler room

25. Which of the following sprinkler-head orientations are available recessed and surface mounted?
    a. Pendant and sidewall
    b. Upright and pendant
    c. Concealed and sidewall
    d. Upright and concealed

CHAPTER 7. Plumbing and Mechanical Requirements

1. Plumbing requirements are found in the building code and the plumbing code. **True/False**

2. The general rule for plumbing fixtures is that every floor in a building will require at least two restrooms. **True/False**

3. In larger restrooms, there are usually more lavatories than water closets. **True/False**

4. Plumbing, mechanical, and electrical systems are often planned simultaneously during a design project. **True/False**

5. The mechanical codes are the only resource for mechanical requirements. **True/False**

6. A mechanical room is not typically required to meet accessibility requirements. **True/False**

7. On smaller plumbing projects where an engineer is not required by the codes, a licensed _____ can do the work directly from your drawings.

8. All plumbing fixtures must have a smooth, _____ finish.

9. If a urinal is required in a project, it is usually substituted for a required _____.

10. What is the maximum depth of an accessible kitchen or breakroom sink in inches or millimeters? _____

11. HVAC stands for heating, _____, and air conditioning.

12. The cooling _____ refers to how much energy is required to cool a space.

13. Which of the following is tied to the plumbing system of a building and may involve the services of a plumbing engineer if required on a project?
    a. Standpipes
    b. Sprinklers
    c. Drinking fountains
    d. b and c only
    e. All of the above

14. What is the first item you need to determine when you are planning the layout of a toilet facility?
    a. The occupancy classification
    b. The type of fixtures required
    c. The number of fixtures required
    d. The actual number of occupants

15. Which of the following statements about plumbing fixtures is *not* correct?
    a. Urinals are not always required in a male restroom.
    b. Travel distance can limit the number of fixtures that can be grouped together.
    c. If a tenant space has its own toilet, it can be deducted from the total facilities required for that floor.
    d. Some smaller occupancies allow one toilet facility, as long as it is unisex and accessible.
    e. All of the above are correct.

16. Which of the following statements about accessible toilet facilities is *not* correct?
    a. A single accessible toilet facility may be allowed in some existing buildings.
    b. Separate toilet facilities must typically be provided for employees and customers.
    c. When a building has multiple toilet facilities, a percentage of them must be accessible.
    d. In an apartment complex, some of the apartments must have accessible toilet facilities.
    e. When urinals are provided in a toilet facility at least one typically needs to be accessible.

17. Which of the following statements about required unisex facilities is *not* correct?
    a. Certain occupancies are required to have a unisex bathing facility.
    b. Unisex toilet facilities are sometimes referred to as family facilities.
    c. A unisex toilet facility is usually required if more than eight water closets are provided.
    d. Any required unisex facility is counted in the total number of plumbing fixtures.
    e. All of the above are correct.

18. Which of the following plumbing requirements is *not* controlled by the ADA guidelines?
    a. Ease of control
    b. Minimum clearances
    c. Reach heights
    d. Finish of fixture

19. What is the typical accessible distance required between the centerline of a water closet and the side wall?
    a. 10 inches (255 mm)
    b. 15 inches (381 mm)
    c. 18 inches (455 mm)
    d. 24 inches (610 mm)

20. Urinals are most commonly used in which occupancy classifications?
    a. Assembly and Educational occupancies
    b. Assembly and Mercantile occupancies
    c. Mercantile and Institutional occupancies
    d. Educational and Institutional occupancies

21. Which of the following statements about drinking fountains is *not* correct?
    a. A drinking fountain cannot be installed in the vestibule leading to a restroom.
    b. At least one drinking fountain in each floor must be accessible.
    c. The location of the water spout in the drinking fountain is based on whether the approach is from the front or from the side.
    d. The front edge of a drinking fountain can never protrude more than 4 inches (100 mm) past the face of the adjacent wall.
    e. All of the above are correct.

22. All accessible toilet facilities must have a turning circle with a minimum diameter of:
    a. 48 inches (1220 mm)
    b. 60 inches (1525 mm)
    c. 66 inches (1675 mm)
    d. 72 inches (1830 mm)

23. Which of the following statements is correct?
    a. Bathtubs are required by the codes in a wide variety of occupancies.
    b. The swing of the door to an accessible toilet stall does not affect the size of the stall.
    c. The codes control the shape of the seat on a water closet.
    d. Accessible sinks require more clear kneespace than accessible lavatories.

24. If you were designing the layout of a multiple-toilet facility, which of the following would *not* meet codes?
    a. Adding a vestibule before you get to the restroom door
    b. Locating a drinking fountain in the vestibule leading to the restroom
    c. Using plastic laminate toilet stalls
    d. Mounting all toilet accessories at accessible heights

25. The typical floor clearance required at most accessible plumbing fixtures and accessories is:
    a. 30 by 40 inches (760 by 1015 mm)
    b. 36 by 40 inches (915 by 1015 mm)
    c. 30 by 48 inches (760 by 1220 mm)
    d. 36 by 48 inches (915 by 1220 mm)

26. Showers are most often used in which occupancy classifications?
    a. Institutional, Educational, and Assembly occupancies
    b. Educational, Residential, and Industrial occupancies
    c. Residential, Educational, and Assembly occupancies
    d. Assembly, Residential, and Institutional occupancies

27. Which of the following statements about bathing facilities is *not* correct?
    a. The codes require the walls surrounding the shower to be a minimum of 70 inches (1778 mm) above the shower drain.
    b. A curb at a shower stall cannot be higher than .25 inches (6.4 mm).
    c. A unisex bathing facility must include a lavatory and a water closet in addition to the bathtub or shower.
    d. An accessible lavatory is sometimes allowed within the clear floor space of a roll-in shower.
    e. All of the above are correct.

28. The International Symbol of Accessibility should be included on a sign when it is posted at the following locations:
    a. On the door of an accessible toilet stall
    b. At the entrance to an accessible toilet facility
    c. At the entrance to a nonaccessible toilet facility
    d. a and b only
    e. All of the above

29. When working with mechanical systems, suspended ceilings are often used because:
    a. They provide easy access to ductwork.
    b. They allow access to fire dampers.
    c. They create a shaft plenum.
    d. a and b only
    e. All of the above

30. Which of the following does *not* affect the cooling load of a space?
    a. Exterior windows
    b. Light fixtures
    c. People
    d. a and b only
    e. All of the above affect cooling load.

31. Which of the following statements about plenum air systems is *not* correct?
    a. Only certain types of wiring are allowed in the plenum space.
    b. No ducts are required in the plenum space.
    c. Use of combustible materials is not allowed in the plenum space.
    d. They are limited to specific fire areas within a building.
    e. All of the above are correct.

32. When designing a mechanical system which of the following scenarios would *not* typically be zoned separately from the rest of the space?
    a. A small office within the interior space of an accounting firm
    b. A kitchen in a Mexican restaurant
    c. The main conference room in a large law firm
    d. A computer room in a high school

33. A registered mechanical engineer is not always legally required on an interiors project. It depends on:
    a. The size of the project
    b. The amount of mechanical work to be done
    c. The code jurisdiction of the project
    d. a and b only
    e. All of the above

34. Energy efficiency can be affected by which of the following building systems?
    a. Lighting systems
    b. Plumbing systems
    c. Mechanical systems
    d. a and c only
    e. All of the above

❑ CHAPTER 8. Electrical and Communication Requirements

1. The *National Electrical Code* does not regulate public telephones.   **True/False**

2. Most occupancy classifications require noncombustible electrical cables to be installed.   **True/False**

3. Outlet boxes are electrical boxes installed primarily in walls and floors.   **True/False**

4. The terms *emergency electrical system* and *standby power system* mean the same thing.   **True/False**

5. AFCI circuits are only required at wall receptacles in sleeping rooms.   **True/False**

6. A lock is considered to be fail safe if the door automatically unlocks in an emergency.   **True/False**

7. Metal clad cable is different from BX cable because it has an extra _____ wire.

8. In residential occupancies, receptacle outlet boxes must be installed so that no point along the horizontal floor line is more than how many feet or millimeters from an outlet? _____

9. When an emergency electrical system takes over from the main power source during an emergency, the delay typically cannot be longer than _____ seconds.

10. Communication systems are not heavily regulated by the codes because the wiring has lower _____ than electrical systems.

11. Most code requirements for electrical systems are found in which of the following publications?
    a. *NEMA 70*
    b. *NFPA 70*
    c. *ASTM 70*
    d. *ANSI 70*

12. When a designer works with an electrical engineer on a project, which of the following will often be done by the designer?
    a. Determine the location of the electrical outlets.
    b. Determine the types of electrical cables.
    c. Determine the size of the electrical load.
    d. Determine the placement of electrical cables.

13. Which of the following may be determined by an electrical engineer?
    a. Smoke detectors
    b. Fire alarms
    c. Light fixtures
    d. b and c only
    e. All of the above

14. Which of the following types of electrical panels are used to supply electricity to each floor within a building?
    a. Power panel board
    b. Branch panel board
    c. Power switchboard
    d. Branch switchboard

15. Which type of cable is often used to connect light fixtures in a suspended ceiling grid?
    a. Flex cable
    b. Romex cable
    c. Metal clad cable
    d. Flat wire

16. When an electrical cable passes through a fire barrier, the codes typically require the use of which of the following?
    a. Smokestop
    b. Fire damper
    c. Cover plate
    d. Firestop

17. Which of the following occupancies are typically *not* allowed by the codes to use flat wire?
    a. Assembly, Detentional, and Educational occupancies
    b. Educational, Residential, and Detentional occupancies
    c. Health Care, Educational, and Residential occupancies
    d. Health Care, Educational, and Mercantile occupancies

18. Which type of cabling is limited mostly to residential occupancies?
    a. Romex cable
    b. Flex cable
    c. Metal clad cable
    d. Flat wire cable

19. To make a wall outlet accessible, the bottom of the outlet box must be mounted a minimum of how far from the floor?
    a. 12 inches (305 mm)
    b. 15 inches (380 mm)
    c. 20 inches (510 mm)
    d. 24 inches (610 mm)

20. Which of the following statements about light fixtures is *not* correct?
    a. Light fixtures over 50 pounds typically need a stronger electrical box.
    b. Any type of tested light fixture is allowed in a fire rated ceiling assembly.
    c. All light fixtures must be placed to allow easy access for future repairs and wire changes.
    d. Only labeled light fixtures can be installed on the interior of a building.
    e. All of the above are correct.

21. In which of the following areas would a GFCI outlet *not* be required?
    a. Adjacent to a dwelling unit restroom lavatory
    b. General wall outlet in a public restroom
    c. Adjacent to a dwelling unit wet bar
    d. General wall outlet in a dwelling unit kitchen

22. If an electrical device passes through a rated wall assembly, the opening around the device cannot be more than:
    a. 1/16 inch (1.6 mm)
    b. 1/8 inch (3 mm)
    c. 1/4 inch (6.4 mm)
    d. 3/8 inch (9.6 mm)

23. Which of the following statements about circuitry is *not* correct?
    a. A circuit feeds electricity to an electrical item and returns back to the panel board.
    b. Codes limit the number of volts or amperage on a single circuit.
    c. A circuit can affect the number of light fixtures on one switch.
    d. Circuits organize and distribute electricity within a building.
    e. All of the above are correct.

24. Which of the following statements about conduit is *not* correct?
    a. Conduit is always made of metal.
    b. A conduit can carry multiple wires.
    c. Conduit can act as a ground.
    d. Codes sometimes limit the length of conduit.
    e. All of the above are correct.

25. Which of the following components is used when you want to terminate electrical wires for future use?
    a. Conduit body
    b. Receptacle outlet
    c. Junction box
    d. None of the above

26. Which of the following electrical code and accessibility requirements is *not* correct?
    a. Hanging (pendant) light fixtures are not allowed in bathing rooms.
    b. Metal and plastic electrical raceways can be used to distribute electrical cables.
    c. The size of an electrical box in a rated wall is typically limited to 16 square inches (10,300 sq mm).
    d. Only wall sconces deeper than 4 inches (100 mm) must be mounted over 80 inches (2032 mm) above the floor.
    e. All of the above are correct.

27. Which of the following statements about an emergency electrical system is *not* correct?
    a. Exit signs are often connected to an emergency electrical system.
    b. Artificial lighting must be present in exit discharges when the building is in use.
    c. Life-support equipment in hospitals is often connected to an emergency electrical system.
    d. Typically emergency lighting must last at least 1½ hours after power failure.
    e. All of the above are correct.

28. Which of the following occupancies is usually required by the codes and the ADA guidelines to have an assistive listening system?
    a. Assembly occupancy
    b. Health Care occupancy
    c. Industrial occupancy
    d. Educational occupancy

29. Which of the following are considered part of a communication system?
    a. Intercoms
    b. Telephones
    c. Background music
    d. Security
    e. a and b only
    f. All of the above

30. Which of the following statements is *not* correct?
    a. Most telecommunication rooms contain computer equipment.
    b. Most telecommunication rooms must be separated from the rest of the building by rated assemblies.
    c. Telecommunication rooms must meet requirements found in the *NEC* and other industry standards.
    d. Communication and satellite closets must meet requirements similar to telecommunication rooms.
    e. All of the above are correct.

31. Match each of the unique characteristics on the right with the type of communication cable shown on the left.
    ___ Fiber optic cables   a. Commonly used for video transmissions
    ___ Twisted pair cables   b. Uses transmitters to connect users to system
    ___ Wireless   c. Bundles various types of cables into one sleeve
    ___ Zone cabling   d. Are divided into different categories
    ___ Coaxial cables   e. Provides the highest speed and capacity
    ___ Composite cables   f. Uses intermediate terminals in ceilings

32. Which of the following communication cabling requirements is correct?
    a. Low-voltage cabling run above a suspended ceiling must be in cable trays.
    b. All old low-voltage cabling that is abandoned must be removed.
    c. Low-voltage cables run in ceiling plenums must typically be rated for plenums.
    d. Electrical and low-voltage wiring are typically run together in the same conduit.
    e. All of the above are correct.

CHAPTER 9. Finish and Furniture Selection

1. The *Smolder Resistance Test* is also known as the *Cigarette Ignition Test*.   True/False

2. *DOC FFl-70* and *DOC FF2-70* are two different types of *Pitts Test*.   True/False

3. If you found an antique sofa, you could have it tested and use it in a space
    that requires its seating to pass *CAL133*.   True/False

4. Paint applied to a surface does not have to be rated because it is considered
    thermally thin.   True/False

5. As you travel through a means of egress toward the exit discharge, the required
    finish classes become stricter.   True/False

6. If a finish is not pretested, there is no way you can use it on a project.   True/False

7. A fire _____ is a separate material that may be used underneath an upholstery
    fabric on a chair or sofa for the purpose of creating a fire barrier.

8. _____ occurs when a fire generates so much heat that the combustible
    materials in the room reach their ignition temperature and simultaneously ignite.

9. A(n) _____ company can add a fire retardant coating to a finish to make it more
    flame resistant.

10. Accessibility requirements for furniture usually apply to two types of furniture: seating and

    _____ .

11. Match each test name on the left with the number designation shown on the right. Fill in the
    appropriate letter on the lines shown.

    ___ *Pill Test*   a. *NFPA 265*

    ___ *Steiner Tunnel Test*   b. *DOC FF1-70*

    ___ *Vertical Flame Test*   c. *ASTM E648*

    ___ *Radiant Panel Test*   d. *NFPA 260*

    ___ *Room Corner Test*   e. *NFPA 701*

    ___ *Toxicity Test*   f. *NFPA 269*

    ___ *Smolder Resistance Test*   g. *DOC FF4-72*

    ___ *Mattress Test*   h. *ASTM E84*

12. Which of the following finish tests is a rated test and *not* a pass/fail test?
    a. *Vertical Flame Test*
    b. *Radiant Panel Test*
    c. *Room Corner Test*
    d. *Pill Test*

13. Which of the following tests is required for mattresses used in certain Institutional occupancies?
    a. *DOC FF4-72*
    b. *CAL 117*
    c. *ASTM E1590*
    d. *NFPA 272*

14. Which of the following tests would *not* typically be used on the upholstery of a chair?
    a. *Steiner Tunnel Test*
    b. *CAL 133*
    c. *Radiant Panel Test*
    d. *Smolder Resistance Test*

15. The *Pitts Test* is typically used to test which of the following?
    a. Finishes
    b. Mattresses
    c. Conduit
    d. a and b only
    e. All of the above

16. Which of the following does *not* typically affect which finish test is required on a project?
    a. The size of the building
    b. Where the finish is applied
    c. The type of occupancy classification
    d. The jurisdiction of the project

17. Which of the following statements about *CAL 133* is *not* correct?
    a. The test consists of setting a whole piece of furniture on fire.
    b. The aim of the test is to eliminate the flashover that occurs in the second phase of a fire.
    c. All jurisdictions in the United States enforce *CAL 133* requirements.
    d. It is a pass/fail test.
    e. b and c
    f. All of the above are correct.

18. Which of the following is *not* a *Room Corner Test*?
    a. *UL 1715*
    b. *NFPA 265*
    c. *NFPA 286*
    d. *NFPA 253*

19. A fabric is considered flame resistant if it does which of the following?
    a. Resists catching on fire
    b. Chars instead of burns
    c. Terminates the flame after the ignition source is removed
    d. a and c only
    e. All of the above

20. Which of the following finish tests would be used on a tufted fabric applied to a wall?
    a. *Room Corner Test*
    b. *Steiner Tunnel Test*
    c. *Radiant Panel Test*
    d. *Smolder Resistance Test*

21. Which of the following finish tests uses a cigarette and measures the char mark created to determine if a fabric passes or fails?
    a. *NFPA 701*
    b. *NFPA 269*
    c. *NFPA 265*
    d. *NFPA 260*

22. Which of the following finish tests measures both how fast a flame will spread and how much smoke is created?
    a. *Room Corner Test*
    b. *Steiner Tunnel Test*
    c. *Radiant Panel Test*
    d. *Toxicity Test*

23. Which of the following finish tests is typically used on vertical finishes exposed to air on both sides?
    a. *CAL 116*
    b. *UL 723*
    c. *ASTM E648*
    d. *NFPA 701*

24. If you are planning to have a fire-retardant finish added to some fabric for a drapery treatment, you may decide to have a sample tested first because:
    a. The fabric is a special blend, and you want to make sure the fabric will not shrink.
    b. The fabric has a texture, and you want to make sure the texture will not flatten.
    c. The fabric has a bold pattern, and you want to make sure the colors will not bleed into each other.
    d. b and c only
    e. All of the above

25. Which of the following occupancy classifications tend to have the strictest finish and furniture code requirements?
    a. Residential, Health Care, and Assembly occupancies
    b. Educational, Assembly, and Health Care occupancies
    c. Detentional/Correctional, Assembly, and Educational occupancies
    d. Health Care, Detentional/Correctional, and Residential occupancies

26. Which of the following statements is *not* correct?
    a. A building with an automatic sprinkler system will not typically require rated finishes.
    b. When a finish is applied to furring strips, the intervening spaces must either be filled with a fire rated material or be fire blocked.
    c. Mirrors are not allowed on or adjacent to an exit door.
    d. Glass used as an interior finish will be required to meet safety glazing requirements if used in certain locations.
    e. All of the above are correct.

27. Which type of finish may be affected by the *10 percent rule*?
    a. Crown molding
    b. Cellular plastic
    c. Wall hanging
    d. a and c only
    e. All of the above

28. Which of the following would typically have the strictest finish requirements?
    a. Exit stair
    b. Executive office
    c. Exit access corridor
    d. Conference room

29. For a worksurface or counter to be accessible the height must allow a clear kneespace of:
    a. 24 inches (610 mm)
    b. 27 inches (685 mm)
    c. 28 inches (710 mm)
    d. 30 inches (760 mm)

30. Which of the following flooring situations would least likely meet typical accessibility requirements?
    a. A detectable warning in the floor at the top of a ramp
    b. A carpet installed with a thin double-stick pad
    c. A slip-resistant floor finish in a shower room
    d. A marble floor butting up to a carpet with no pad

31. The *Smolder Resistant Tests NFPA 261, CAL 117,* and *ASTM 1352* were developed specifically to test which of the following?
    a. Fabrics
    b. Mock-ups
    c. Drapes
    d. Foams

32. Which of the following statements about the symbols created by the Association for Contract Textiles (ACT) is *not* correct?
    a. They set standards for upholstery, wallcoverings, upholstered walls, drapery, and furniture.
    b. They are used voluntarily by textile manufacturers.
    c. They indicate a textile's characteristics in colorfastness, abrasion, flame resistance, and other physical properties.
    d. They indicate the standard test the item must meet in order to bear the symbol.
    e. All of the above are correct.

33. Since the designer can be held liable for a project even after it is completed, which of the following is *not* a good finish and furniture selection practice for liability reasons?
    a. Strictly following the requirements of your jurisdiction.
    b. Keep all of your research organized and with the rest of the project information.
    c. Make photocopies of all code sections that apply to your project.
    d. Maintain a code checklist indicating the standards used for each project.
    e. All of the above are good practices.

CHAPTER 10. Code Officials and the Code Process

1. A permit must be obtained for all interior projects.   **True/False**

2. A code requirement can have more than one interpretation.   **True/False**

3. When a code discrepancy is brought to the Board of Appeals, the Board has the authority to disagree and waive that code requirement.   **True/False**

4. During the preliminary design, you should typically get the appropriate federal agency to review your plans for compliance to federal laws.   **True/False**

5. An authority having jurisdiction can include a code jurisdiction, a code _____, and a code _____.

6. A(n) _____ must be clearly posted at the job site during construction.

7. Code research should typically begin during the _____ phase of the design process.

8. A permit is typically obtained from the codes department by a(n) _____.

9. Code research should be documented in project files, construction drawings, and/or _____.

10. Which of the following code officials will review your construction drawings during both the preliminary review and the final review?
    a. Building inspector
    b. Plans examiner
    c. Fire marshal
    d. b and c
    e. All of the above

11. What is the first step in determining which codes to use on a project?
    a. To determine which edition is being used
    b. To determine in which jurisdiction the project is located
    c. To determine if any local amendments have been made
    d. To determine what is required for final code approval

12. Which of the following steps in the code process is *not* typically done by the designer?
    a. Code research
    b. Permit process
    c. Appeals process
    d. Preliminary review

13. Which of the following scenarios would typically *not* require a permit?
    a. Reconfiguring one wall to enlarge an existing office
    b. Replacing an existing HVAC system on the third floor of a building
    c. Replacing the wallpaper in a retirement center
    d. Adding a demising wall to create a new tenant space
    e. All of the above would require a permit.

14. A preliminary code review of your drawings should be done with a code official during which stage of the design process?
    a. Programming phase
    b. Design phase
    c. Schematic phase
    d. Construction drawing phase

15. Which of the following would be a valid reason to try to obtain an appeal for an interior project?
    a. The conditions in an existing building will not allow you to fully meet a code requirement.
    b. A particular code requirement is going to be very costly and you want to use an alternate solution.
    c. You and the code official(s) in your jurisdiction cannot agree on an interpretation of one of the codes required for your project.
    d. a and c only
    e. All of the above

16. Which of the following statements is true?
    a. When the Board of Appeals grants your appeal, it can be used on future projects as long as the same code scenario occurs.
    b. If you take your drawings through the preliminary review process, you will be allowed to skip the permit review process.
    c. A tenant can occupy a space if a Temporary Certificate of Occupancy has been issued by a code official.
    d. To obtain a permit, the construction documents must be stamped by a licensed professional.

17. Which of the following is *not* a typical code inspection required on an interior project?
    a. Final inspection
    b. Footing inspection
    c. Framing inspection
    d. Penetration inspection
    e. b and c

18. Why does a code official inspect a project during construction?
    a. The code official makes sure the work complies with the codes.
    b. Inspection ensures that a Certificate of Occupancy can be issued.
    c. Inspections during construction guarantee that the work matches the construction documents.
    d. a and b
    e. All of the above

19. Which of the following would *not* be a reason to use a performance code in a project?
    a. The client wants to try to avoid having to pay for the addition of a fire wall so you want to use an alternate wall assembly.
    b. A new sustainable product just became available and you want to use it in place of a material suggested by the codes.
    c. You want to build all the corridor walls out of transparent plastic, but some of the walls are required to be fire rated and you have an alternate solution.
    d. An existing building will not allow you to meet all the typical means of egress requirements without costly changes, so you want to enhance the extinguishing system.
    e. All of the above are correct.

20. Which of the following statements about the documentation of performance requirements is *not* correct?
   a. The performance-related requirements should be clearly delineated from the perspective code requirements.
   b. During plans review the documentation is always reviewed by an outside consultant known as a contract reviewer.
   c. The documentation will typically include more than just the construction drawings and specifications.
   d. It will often require a review process separate from the perspective code part of the project.
   e. All of the above are correct.

SECTION 3

STUDY PROBLEMS

☐ CHAPTER 1. About the Codes

Problem 1

Chapter 1 discusses the main code organizations, standards organizations, and federal agencies as they relate to interior projects. Fill in as many as you can remember in the spaces provided. Show full names and acronyms.

Code Organizations:

1. _____

2. _____

Standards Organizations:

1. _____

2. _____

3. _____

4. _____

5. _____

Federal Departments:

1. _____

2. _____

3. _____

PROBLEM 2

In the spaces provided, fill in the full code, standard name, or federal regulation based on the acronym shown below:

ABA _____

ADA _____

FHA _____

IBC _____

ICC/ANSI _____

ICCEC _____

ICCPC _____

IEBC _____

IECC _____

IFC _____

IMC _____

IPC _____

IRC _____

LSC _____

NEC _____

UFAS _____

UFC _____

UMC _____

UPC _____

❑ CHAPTER 2. Occupancy Classifications and Loads

PROBLEM 1

Refer to the chart, "Comparison of Occupancy Classifications," in Appendix A.1 (or Figure 2.2 in the *Guidebook*) for this problem. The chart lists all the occupancy classifications for the *International Building Code (IBC)* and the NFPA codes including the *NFPA 5000* and *Life Safety Code (LSC)*.

Based on this chart, answer the following questions concerning occupancy classifications. Write your answers in the spaces provided.

a. If you were asked to design the interior of a prison located in a jurisdiction using the *IBC*, which occupancy classification would you use? _____

b. Using the *NFPA 5000*, which occupancy classification would you use if you were asked to redesign the interior of a hotel? _____

c. A client asks you to select finishes for a nightclub that he owns. Based on the *LSC*, what additional information do you need in order to determine the correct occupancy classification? _____

d. If you are designing the interior of a restaurant that seats a maximum of 65 people and you are using the *IBC*, which occupancy classification would you use?_____
Why? _____
_____
_____

e. If you are selecting finishes for the same restaurant using the *LSC*, which occupancy classification would you use? _____
Why? _____
_____
_____

PROBLEM 2

Refer to the *International Building Code (IBC)* Table 1004.1.2, "Maximum Floor Area Allowances Per Occupant," in Appendix A.2 (or Figure 2.8 in the *Guidebook*) for this problem.

Based on the *IBC* Table 1004.1.2, determine the occupant load for the floor plan shown in Figure 2.1. The plan is a retail clothing store on the first floor (at grade level) of a strip mall. Use the occupant load formula to determine the occupant load for this store and write your answer in the space provided. (The metric conversion variable is given at the bottom of the code table.)

Occupant load of Figure 2.1 = _____

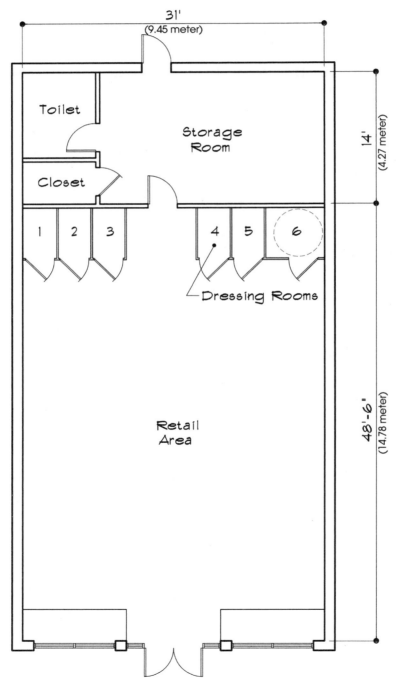

Figure 2.1. Occupant Load: Retail Store

PROBLEM 3

Refer to the *International Building Code (IBC)* Table 1004.1.2, "Maximum Floor Area Allowances Per Occupant," in Appendix A.2 (or Figure 2.8 in the *Guidebook*) and what you know about the codes for this problem.

a. Figure 2.2 indicates the floor plans of four single-story buildings. In which plan could the Storage occupancy (S) or use be considered an accessory to the main occupancy classification? Write the letter of the plan selected in the space provided and explain your answer. _____
Explain: _____

_____

b. Based on the *IBC* Table 1004.1.2, determine the total occupant load for the building in Plan A of Figure 2.2. with the Educational and Storage uses. The Educational (E) use is primarily classrooms. Write your answer in the space provided. (The metric conversion variable is given at the bottom of the code table.)

Occupant load of Figure 2.2A = _____

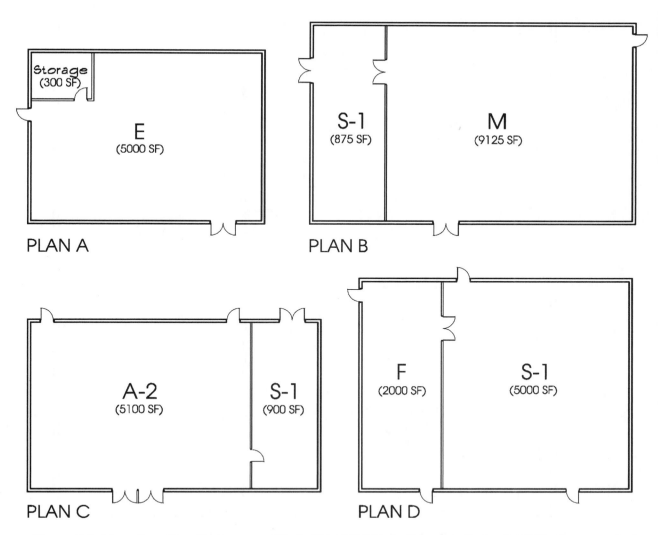

Figure 2.2. More than One Occupancy: Single-Story Buildings (1 square foot = 0.0929 square meter)

PROBLEM 4

Refer to the *International Building Code* Table 1004.1.2, "Maximum Floor Area Allowances Per Occupant," in Appendix A.2 (or Figure 2.8 in the *Guidebook*) for this problem.

The building indicated in Figure 2.3 is a college building that includes an Assembly Hall, a Library and Administrative Offices. It also includes toilet facilities and a small amount of storage for use by the Assembly Hall and the Library. The central Student Lounge area is used with tables and chairs as a study or eating space. Using what you know about occupant loads determine the occupant load of the Student Lounge. Write you answer in the space provided. (The metric conversion variable is given at the bottom of the code table.)

Occupant load of Figure 2.3 =_____

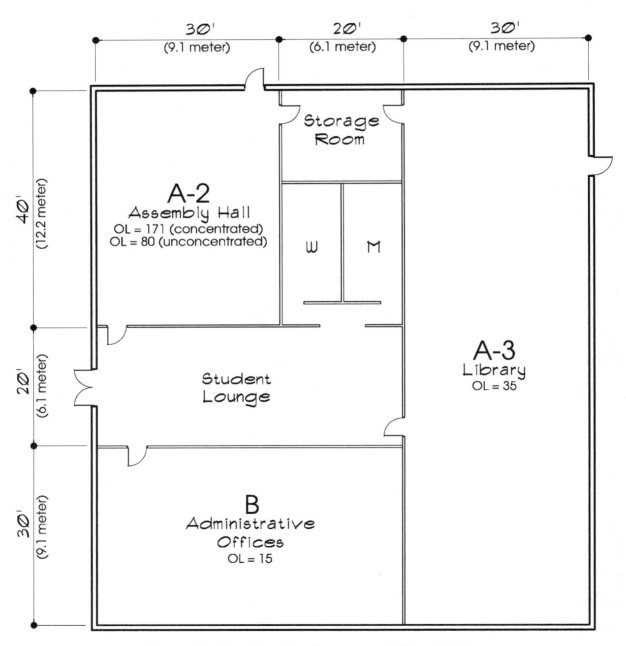

Figure 2.3. More than One Occupancy: College Building

PROBLEM 5

Refer to the *International Building Code* Table 1004.1.2, "Maximum Floor Area Allowances Per Occupant," in Appendix A.2 (or Figure 2.8 in the *Guidebook*) for this problem.

a. Based on this table, determine the occupant load for the church in the floor plan shown in Figure 2.4. The seating shown consists of continuous wooden pews bolted to the floor. All pews are the same size: 14'-6" (4419.6 mm) long. This includes the 3-inch (76.2 mm) wide arms on each end. Write your answer in the space provided.

Occupant load of Figure 2.4 = _____

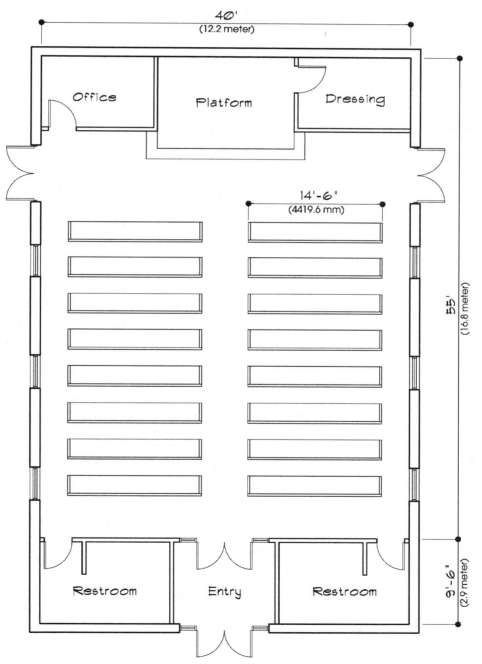

Figure 2.4. Fixed Seating: Church with Pews

b. Using the same floor plan in Figure 2.4, determine the occupant load for the church if all the pews have dividing arms. An example of one of the pews is shown in Figure 2.5. A dividing arm separates each seat, and eight (8) people can sit in each pew. Write your answer in the space provided.

Occupant load of Figure 2.4 with dividing arms = _____

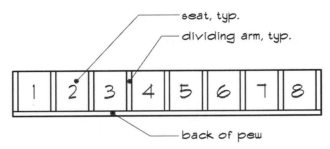

Figure 2.5. Fixed Seating: Divided Pews

PROBLEM 6

Refer to the *International Building Code* Table 1004.1.2, "Maximum Floor Area Allowances Per Occupant," in Appendix A.2 (or Figure 2.8 in the *Guidebook*) for this problem.

A developer recently purchased a vacant building, an old high school that closed more than 10 years ago. You are working with a team to help the developer determine how to develop the building. There are two floors, each floor is 4600 square feet (427.34 s m), for a total of 9200 gross square feet (854.7 s m). Using the occupant load formula and the code table indicated above, determine which of the following three scenarios will be allowed by the codes. Give a yes or no answer and explain how you obtained your answer in the spaces provided. (The metric conversion variable is given at the bottom of the code table.)

a. The developer is considering an apartment complex. He wants to divide the building into 4 one-person units, 8 four-person units, and 3 six-person units. Based on the occupant load, will this work? _____

Explain: _____

_____

_____

b. The developer is considering turning the building into a retirement center that provides minimum health services. He plans to house 62 tenants and expects 8 full-time employees. Based on the occupant load, will this work?_____

Explain: _____

_____

_____

c. The developer is also considering a two-story retail center with stores open to the public on both floors. He expects an occupant load of 125 on the first floor and 85 on the second floor. Based on the occupant load, will this work?_____

Explain: _____

_____

_____

☐ CHAPTER 3. Construction Types and Building Sizes

PROBLEM 1

Refer to the *International Building Code* Table 601, "Fire-Resistance Rating Requirements for Building Elements," in Appendix A.3 (or Figure 3.1 in the *Guidebook*) for this problem.

Based on this code table, answer each of the questions listed below. Fill in your answers in the spaces provided.

a. What does the designation of A and B indicate in this chart? _____

   _____

b. What is the typical fire-resistance rating for columns that are part of the structural frame in a Type VA building?_____

c. What is the typical fire-resistance rating for an interior bearing wall within a Type IIA building? _____

d. Which construction type requires a 2-hour fire rating for its floor construction? _____

   _____

e. According to this table, what structure or building element does not typically require a fire rating? _____

PROBLEM 2

Refer to the *International Building Code* Table 503, "Allowable Height and Building Areas," in Appendix A.4 (or Figure 3.4 in the *Guidebook*) for this problem as well as the chart "Comparison of Occupancy Classifications" in Appendix A.1 (or Figure 2.2 in the *Guidebook*) if required.

Using this table, determine which of the following scenarios would be allowed by the *IBC*. Give a yes or no answer and explain how you obtained this answer in the spaces provided. Be specific, using your knowledge of occupancy classifications and the information shown in the code table. (A multiplier for metric conversion is given at the bottom of the table.)

a. An existing building with a construction type of Type IIIB has two floors with 17,500 square feet (1626 s m) per floor. Can this building be converted into a hotel?_____

Explain: _____

_____

_____

b. A local developer is planning to develop a series of townhouses. Some will be three stories and some will be four stories. They will all be Type VB construction. The typical first floor will be 3625 square feet (337 s m), the second floor will be 2880 square feet (268 s m), and the third and fourth floor will be 1000 square feet (93 s m) each. Can this be developed as planned according to the IBC?_____

Explain: _____

_____

_____

c. Your client has found a potential building for the relocation of her low-hazard factory. The space is the first floor of an existing two-story building that has a construction type of Type IIIB. Each floor in this building has 19,250 gross square feet (1788 s m). The client expects to expand to have 100 employees. If the occupant load factor for this factory is 100 gross square feet (9.3 s m) per person, will this space work?_____

Explain: _____

_____

_____

CHAPTER 4. Means of Egress

PROBLEM 1

Using the stair diagram shown in Figure 4.1, fill in the typical code requirements for each of the following in the spaces provided. Be sure to indicate whether you are using inches or millimeters. Add the words *minimum* and *maximum* where applicable.

A. Riser height: _____

B. Tread length: _____

C. Nosing projection: _____

D. Stairway rise without landing: _____

E. Height of handrail: _____

F. Top handrail extension: _____

G. Bottom handrail extension: _____

H. Diameter of handrail: _____

I. Minimum ceiling height: _____

J. Minimum headroom height: _____

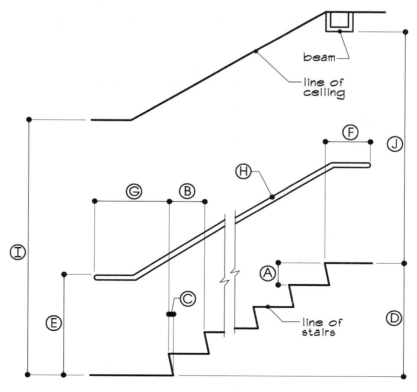

Figure 4.1. Elevation of Stairs

PROBLEM 2

The diagram shown in Figure 4.2 is a line drawing that represents a section of a fully sprinklered high-rise building. It is a new building with the first floor at grade level. You are given the occupant load and the use for each floor. Use the diagram and the information you are given to answer the questions in this two-part problem.

a. Use the occupant load for each floor shown in Figure 4.2, the chart below, and your knowledge of the means of egress codes to determine the number of exits for each floor. List the quantities in the space provided.

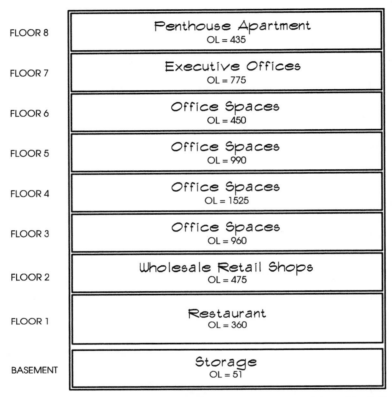

Figure 4.2. Number of Exits: High-Rise Building (sprinklered building)

OCCUPANT LOAD PER STORY/FLOOR	MINIMUM NO. OF EXITS
1–500	2
500–1000	3
Over 1000	4

Basement: _____
First floor: _____
Second floor: _____
Third floor: _____
Fourth floor: _____
Fifth floor: _____
Sixth floor: _____
Seventh floor. _____
Eighth floor: _____

b. Refer to the *International Building Code* Table 1018.2, "Buildings with One Exit" and Table 1014.1, "Spaces with One Means of Egress" in Appendix A.5 (or Figure 4.15 in the *Guidebook*) and Table 1015.1, "Exit Access Travel Distance" in Appendix A.6 (or Figure 4.22 in the *Guidebook*) for this part of the problem.

Answer the following questions using the information shown in the diagram in Figure 4.2 and these two code tables. (Be sure to refer to the notes at the bottom of the code tables.) Note which code table was used to determine your answer. Write your answers in the spaces provided. (A multiplier for metric conversion is given at the bottom of the tables.)

1. What is the maximum travel distance allowed on the first floor?
   Distance: _____
   Code Table: _____

2. If this were a fully sprinklered single-story office building with 35 occupants and one exit, what would be the maximum travel distance allowed?
   Distance: _____
   Code Table: _____

3. What is the maximum travel distance allowed on the second floor in Figure 4.2?
   Distance: _____
   Code Table: _____

4. If these retail shops were located in a two-story building with one exit, what would be the allowable travel distance?
   Distance: _____
   Code Table: _____

5. What is the maximum travel distance allowed on the third through seventh floors in Figure 4.2?
   Distance: _____
   Code Table: _____

PROBLEM 3

Refer to the *International Building Code (IBC)* Table 1005.1, "Egress Width Per Occupant Served," in Appendix A.7 (or Figure 4.17 in the *Guidebook*) for this problem.

Figure 4.3 is a floor plan of the third floor in a four-story building. The third floor has just been totally renovated and includes the installation of a new automatic sprinkler system. Four new tenants plan to occupy the floor. All the tenants are considered Business (B) occupancies. Use the width variables from the *IBC* Table 1005.1 and your knowledge of minimum means of egress widths to answer the following three-part problem. Write your answers in the spaces provided. (A multiplier for metric conversion is given at the bottom of the code table.)

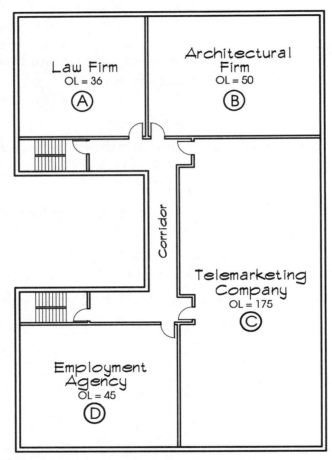

Figure 4.3. Exit Widths: Multi-tenant Building (Third Floor) (sprinklered building)

a. What is the total exit width required for the telemarketing company in Space C? _____
   If the space requires two exits, how wide does each exit or exit door need to be? _____
   Why? _____

   _____

b. What is the total exit width required for each exit stair? _____
   Why? _____

   _____

c. What is the minimum exit width required for the exit access corridor? _____
   Why? _____

   _____

PROBLEM 4

Figure 4.4 shows a table and chair layout for a training room. (It is drawn to scale at 1/8″ = 1′-0.″) Use a straight edge and an architectural scale with this floor plan to determine the answers to the following questions. Using the information given below and the floor plan, determine the minimum required width between the edges of each table at the aisle accessways indicated.

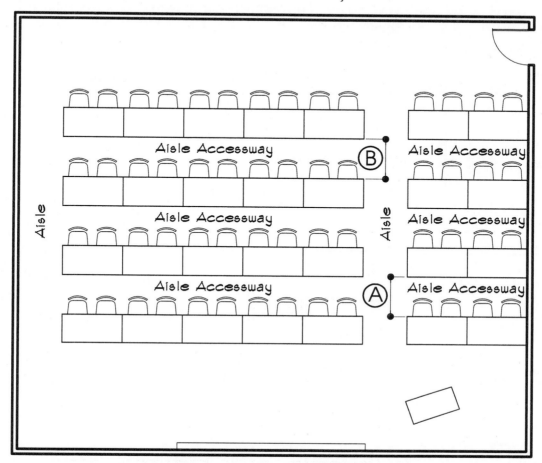

Figure 4.4. Access Aisleway Widths: Training Room (Scale: 1/8″ – 1′-0″)

AISLE ACCESSWAY LENGTH	MINIMUM WIDTH
< 6 feet (1829 mm)	None
6–12 feet (1829–3658 mm)	12 inches (305 mm)
12–30 feet (3658–9144 mm)	12 inches + 0.5(x – 12 feet) or 305 mm + 12.7((x – 3658 mm) ÷ 305)

a. What is the required minimum distance between the tables at Aisle Accessway A? _____
   Explain: _____

   _____

b. What is the required minimum distance between the tables at Aisle Accessway B? _____
   Explain: _____

   _____

PROBLEM 5

Figure 4.5 is a floor plan of a doctor's office1 in a tenant space on the ground floor of a multistory building. The building is unsprinklered. (It is drawn to scale at 1/8″ = 1′-0″.) The only exit from the space is in the waiting area. Use a straight edge and an architectural scale with this floor plan to determine the answers to the following questions. Write your answers in the spaces provided and show how you obtained your answers directly on the floor plan, drawing in lines and dimensions where necessary. Label any lines you draw with the corresponding letter of the question or use a different-colored pencil or highlighter for each question.

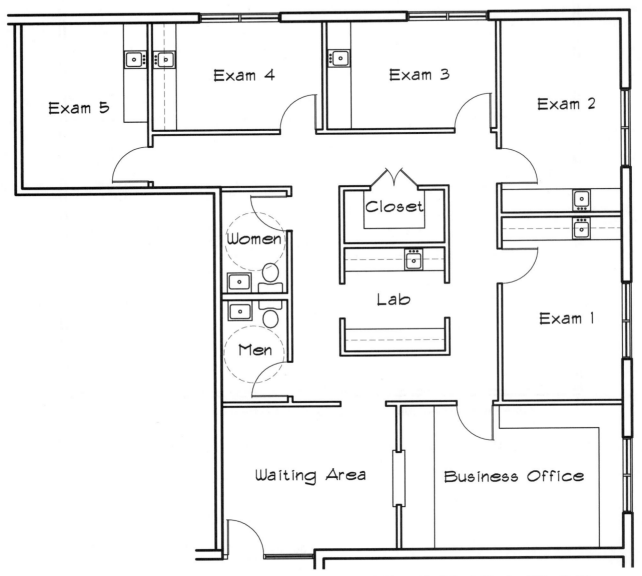

Figure 4.5. Travel Distances: Doctor's Office (nonsprinklered building) (Scale: 1/8″ – 1′-0″)

a. If this space was required to have two exits, what would be the minimum required distance between the two exits? _____

Explain: _____

_____

_____

b. What is the longest travel distance in this space? _____

c. Is there a dead-end corridor in this space? _____ If so, how long is it? _____
Is it allowed? _____
Explain: _____
_____
_____

d. Is there a common path of travel in this space? _____ If so, where is it located?
_____

How long is it? _____

CHAPTER 5. Fire-Resistant Materials and Assemblies

PROBLEM 1

Refer to the *International Building Code (IBC)* Table 302.3.2, "Required Separation of Occupancies (Hours)" in Appendix A.8 (or Figure 5.6 in the *Guidebook*); *IBC* Table 302.1.1, "Incidental Use Areas" in Appendix A.9 (or Figure 5.8 in the *Guidebook*); *IBC* Table 1016.1, "Corridor Fire-Resistance Rating" in Appendix A.10 (or Figure 5.11 in the *Guidebook*) and *IBC* Table 715.3, "Fire Door and Fire Shutter Fire Protection Ratings" in Appendix A.11 (or Figure 5.12 in the *Guidebook*) for this problem. (Use the "Comparison of Occupancy Classifications" chart in Appendix A.1 as required.)

Figure 5.1 is a floor plan of the eighth floor in a 10-story unsprinklered office building. It shows the layout of the building core and five tenant spaces as well as the interior of one tenant space. The tenants are either Business (B) or Mercantile (M) occupancy, as shown on the plan. The legend at the bottom of the floor plan indicates the name of each labeled room or space. Specific wall assemblies on the floor plan are labeled with a circled *letter* designation and certain doors (or opening protectives) are labeled with a circled *number* designation.

Based on the floor plan, the *IBC* tables mentioned above, and your knowledge of the codes, first determine the fire-resistance rating for each of the labeled wall assemblies. Then, for each of the labeled opening protectives, determine the fire-protection rating of the door assembly. Also note any situations where an automatic extinguishing system could be substituted for a rated wall. Write your answers and the code table used in the spaces provided below. If a rating is not required for a particular item, write "no rating" in the space provided, or if a code table is not used, write "no table" in the space provided.

Hourly fire-resistance rating of wall assemblies:

A. Rating: _____ Code Table: _____

B. Rating: _____ Code Table: _____

C. Rating: _____ Code Table: _____

D. Rating: _____ Code Table: _____

E. Rating: _____ Code Table: _____

F. Rating: _____ Code Table: _____

G. Rating: _____ Code Table: _____

H. Rating: _____ Code Table: _____

Hourly fire-protection rating of opening protectives:

1. Rating: _____ Code Table: _____

2. Rating: _____ Code Table: _____

3. Rating: _____ Code Table: _____

4. Rating: _____ Code Table: _____

5. Rating: _____ Code Table: _____

6. Rating: _____ Code Table: _____

7. Rating: _____ Code Table: _____

8. Rating: _____ Code Table: _____

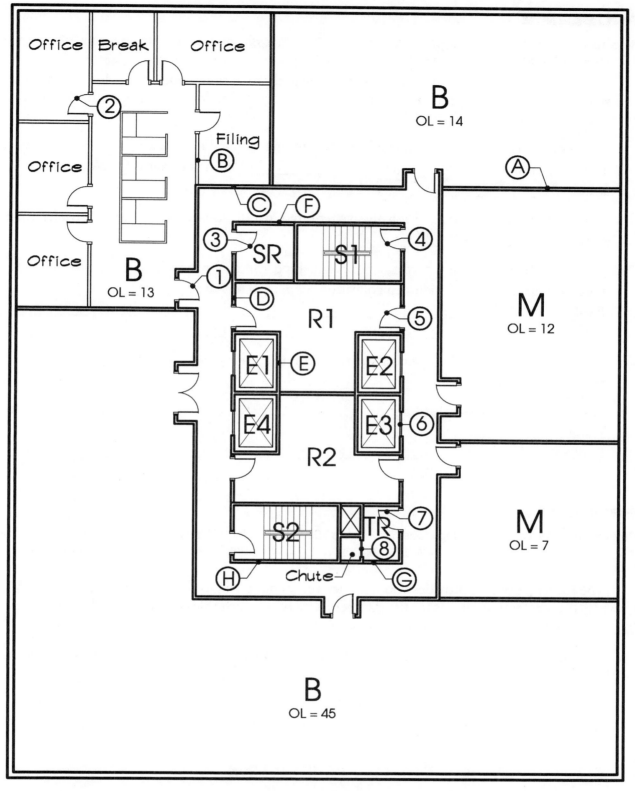

Office Break Office

②

Filing
Ⓑ

Ⓒ Ⓕ

③ SR

S1

④

B
OL = 14

Ⓐ

①

Ⓓ

R1

⑤

E1 Ⓔ E2

E4 E3 ⑥

R2

M
OL = 12

Office

Office

Office

B
OL = 13

S2

TR ⑦

⑧

Ⓗ Chute Ⓖ

M
OL = 7

B
OL = 45

E* = Elevator   SR = Storage Room (150 SF or 14 SM)
R = Restroom   TR = Trash Room (120 SF or 12 SM)
S = Exit Stair   OL = Occupant Load

Figure 5.1. Fire Ratings: Office Building (Eighth Floor) (nonsprinklered building)

PROBLEM 2

Refer to the *International Building Code (IBC)* Table 302.1.1, "Incidental Use Areas" in Appendix A.9 (or Figure 5.8 in the *Guidebook*) for this problem.

This code table provides specific fire separation and protection requirements for special rooms and spaces within a building. Based on the *IBC* table, answer the following questions. Write your answers in the spaces provided.

a. What is the fire rating of a wall in a collection room for soiled linen with an area of 250 square feet (23 s m) in the basement of a hotel? _____ Is an automatic sprinkler system required? _____

b. Is a fire-resistance-rated partition always required in a 110 square foot (10.2 s m) storage room located in a high school? _____

c. Can you substitute an automatic fire-extinguishing system for the 1-hour fire-resistance-rated partitions around waste and linen collection rooms in a hospital? _____
Explain: _____

_____

d. Does a padded cell in a high-security prison require a fire rating?_____ Does it require a sprinkler system?_____

e. Is a 65 square foot (6 s m) storage room in a movie theater required to have a fire suppression system? _____
Explain:_____

_____

PROBLEM 3

Refer to the *International Building Code (IBC)* Table 302.1.1, "Incidental Use Areas" in Appendix A.9 and the *IBC* Table 716.3.1 "Fire Damper Rating," in Appendix A.12 (or Figure 5.8 and 5.16 in the *Guidebook*) for this problem.

The *IBC* Table 302.1.1 provides you with fire-resistance ratings for wall assemblies. Table 716.3.1 provides fire-protection ratings for fire dampers. Use both code tables to answer each of the following questions. Fill in your answers in the spaces provided.

a. Determine the required fire damper rating in a duct that penetrates the partition surrounding a laundry room greater than 100 square feet (9.29 s m) in a hotel. _____

b. Determine the required fire damper rating in a duct that penetrates the partition that separates an incinerator room from an adjacent room. _____

☐ CHAPTER 6. Fire Protection Systems

PROBLEM 1

Automatic sprinkler systems can greatly enhance the fire protection of a building. They can also help to eliminate or reduce other code requirements, since the codes allow automatic sprinkler systems as a "trade-off" for other codes. Quite a few of these trade-offs were listed and/or discussed in Chapter 5 and Chapter 6.

List six of these trade-offs that would affect the interior of a building. Write the answers in the spaces provided below.

1. _____
2. _____
3. _____
4. _____
5. _____
6. _____

PROBLEM 2

In Figure 6.1 are diagrams of six typical sprinkler head orientations. Identify each type.

A. _____
B. _____
C. _____
D. _____
E. _____
F. _____

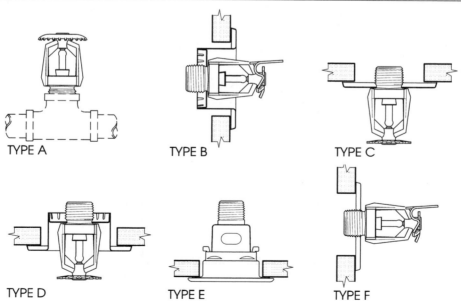

TYPE A

TYPE B

TYPE C

TYPE D

TYPE E

TYPE F

Figure 6.1. Orientation of Sprinkler Heads (Line drawings reprinted with permission from Viking Group (www.vikingcorp.com).)

CHAPTER 7. Plumbing and Mechanical Requirements

PROBLEM 1

The diagram shown in Figure 7.1 represents three elevations of a typical accessible single-toilet facility. The letters indicated in the diagram correspond to the letters listed below. Fill in the typical dimension as required by the codes and accessibility standards for each of the following in the spaces provided. (Indicate the most restrictive requirement.) Be sure to indicate whether you are using inches or millimeters. Add the words *minimum* and *maximum* where applicable.

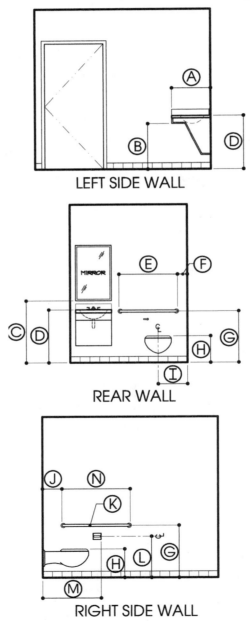

Figure 7.1. Typical Accessible Toilet Elevations

A. Depth of lavatory: _____

B. Height of clear knee space: _____

C. Height to bottom of mirror: _____

D. Height to top of lavatory: _____

E. Length of rear grab bar: _____

F. Distance from side wall to rear grab bar: _____

G. Height to grab bar:_____

H. Height to top of toilet seat: _____

I. Distance from center line of toilet to side wall: _____

J. Distance from rear wall to side grab bar: _____

K. Diameter of grab bar: _____

L. Height to center line of toilet paper dispenser: _____

M. Distance from far side of toilet paper dispenser to rear wall: _____

N. Length of side grab bar:_____

PROBLEM 2

Refer to the *International Plumbing Code* Table 403.1, "Minimum Number of Required Plumbing Fixtures" in Appendix A.13 (or Figure 7.1 in the *Guidebook*) for this problem.

   Answer the questions to the following scenarios based on your knowledge of occupancy classifications and this code table. Fill in the answers and explain how you obtained your answers in the spaces provided.

a. How many water closets are required in a nursing home with an occupant load of 125 for visitors and employees? _____
   Explain:_____
   _____

b. Determine the number of water closets, lavatories, and drinking fountains that would be required for a nightclub with an occupant load of 600.
   Water closets: _____
   Lavatories: _____
   Drinking fountains: _____

c. How many automatic clothes washers are required in a dormitory with an occupant load of 200? _____
   Explain:_____
   _____

d. How many automatic clothes washers are required in an apartment building with 40 dwelling units?_____

e. What are the minimum plumbing requirements for a single-family dwelling? _____
   _____

f. For which gender (male or female) are more water closets required in an opera house?_____
   Explain:_____
   _____

CHAPTER 8. Electrical and Communication Requirements

There are no Study Problems for this chapter.

CHAPTER 9. Finish and Furniture Selection

PROBLEM 1

Refer to the *Life Safety Code (LSC)* Table A.10.2.2, "Interior Finish Classification Limitations," in Appendix A.14 (or Figure 9.14 in the *Guidebook*) for this problem.

The floor plan shown in Figure 9.1 is of the first floor of a five-story hotel. It is an existing building with no sprinkler system. The other four floors are strictly hotel rooms. You have been asked to select all new finishes for this building. Based on the *LSC* Table A.10.2.2 and your knowledge of means of egress, determine which finish class(es) are allowed for each room labeled on the floor plan. The rooms are listed below. Write the finish class(es) in the spaces provided. Include wall and ceiling finish class(es) and any listed floor finish class(es). (*Note:* This building may consist of more than one occupancy classification.)

1. Main Lobby:_____

2. Ballroom: _____

3. Offices:_____

4. Corridor:_____

5. Single Room:_____

6. Suite:_____

7. Vestibule: _____

8. Exit Stair: _____

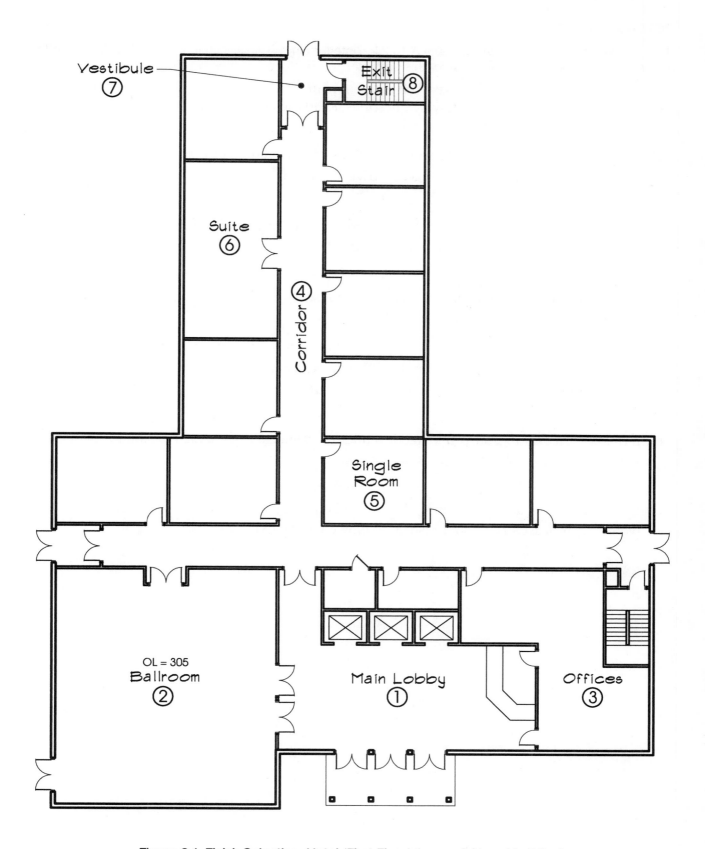

Figure 9.1. Finish Selection: Hotel (First Floor) (nonsprinklered building)

PROBLEM 2

Refer to the *Life Safety Code (LSC)* Table A.10.2.2, "Interior Finish Classification Limitations," in Appendix A.14 (or Figure 9.14 in the *Guidebook*) for this problem.

Below are different scenarios based on the floor plan of the hotel shown in Figure 9.1. Using the *LSC* Table A.10.2.2, answer the following questions. Read each scenario carefully and fill in the correct finish class(es) in the spaces provided.

a. If this was an existing hotel with an automatic sprinkler system instead of being unsprinklered, what would be the least strict wall finish class allowed in the Ballroom?

_____

b. If this was a new, unsprinklered hotel instead of an existing hotel, what wall and flooring finish classes would be allowed in the Exit Stair?

_____

c. If this new unsprinklered hotel had a Gift Shop instead of a Ballroom, what two ceiling finish classes would be allowed in the space?

_____

d. If this was an existing, unsprinklered hospital instead of a hotel, what would be the lowest required finish class allowed in each Patient Room?

_____

e. If this was an existing, unsprinklered juvenile detention facility instead of a hotel, what rating would the floor finishes in the Exit Stair require?

_____

f. If this was a new juvenile detention facility and it had an automatic sprinkler system, what would be the least strict floor finish class allowed in the Exit Stair?

_____

PROBLEM 3

Below are different design scenarios. Based on your knowledge of the variety of tests for interior finishes and furnishings as discussed in Chapter 9, answer the questions in the spaces provided. (*Note:* "No Test" can also be used as an answer.)

a. You found the perfect carpet for the floor of an executive's office in a tenant space. What standard carpet test must this carpet pass? _____

b. You are planning to install this same carpet on the walls in the corridor. What additional test must this carpet pass? _____
   Why? _____
   _____
   _____

c. You have a large tapestry that you are planning to hang in the reception area of a large advertising agency. It covers more than 30 percent of the wall area. What test must this wall hanging pass? _____
   Why? _____
   _____
   _____

d. You are replacing the pleated draperies in the executive office of a brokerage firm. They are floor to ceiling and cover a window wall that extends the full width of the office. What test must the fabric in the new pleated draperies pass? _____
   Why? _____
   _____
   _____

e. You are selecting new seating for a large lobby in a hospital. There will be 3 sofas and 24 upholstered chairs. What test must this seating pass? _____
   Why? _____
   _____
   _____

f. You are working with a lawyer who wants to hang a small fabric wall hanging behind the desk in his office. It covers less than 10 percent of the wall. What test must the wall hanging pass? _____
   Why? _____
   _____
   _____

g. The same client also wants you to select two upholstered guest chairs for his private office. Name two different tests the upholstery on these chairs should pass:
   1. _____
   2. _____

h. A restaurant wants you to select a special fabric to be used in one of its private dining rooms. It will be applied to the ceiling, and it will be tufted. What test must this fabric pass?

_____

Why? _____

_____

_____

i. You are asked to specify mattresses for a hotel. What test must this mattress pass?

_____

Why? _____

_____

_____

☐ CHAPTER 10. Code Officials and the Code Process

There are no Study Problems for this chapter.

SECTION 4

ANSWERS TO SHORT-ANSWER QUESTIONS

☐ CHAPTER 1. About the Codes

1. **True.** There are separate federal requirements that these buildings must follow. Typically, each federal agency sets its own requirements.

2. **True.** Even if two code jurisdictions require the same code and standard publications, they typically create amendments that slightly modify the code and they usually have other requirements, such as municipal ordinances, health codes, and zoning regulations that make their jurisdiction unique.

3. **True.** Many states have chosen to use the *IBC* as a base for their state code. Rather than creating a totally different document, they start with the *International Building Code* and revise certain sections or chapters as needed.

4. **True.** Most jurisdictions use the NFPA *National Electrical Code (NEC)*. The *ICC Electrical Code* only provides administrative provisions as necessary to enforce the *NEC*.

5. **False.** ADA is not a code. It is a civil rights law that protects against discrimination because of disability. It covers many aspects such as employment, communication, transportation, services, and the design of public buildings.

6. **True.** Standards must be referenced by a code publication or formally adopted by a jurisdiction to have legal standing.

7. **True.** Sometimes, stricter requirements are better for the client and/or the safety of the occupants.

8. **False.** Typically, a performance code will apply to only one part or aspect of the project and prescriptive codes will be used to design the rest of the project.

9. **False.** Only the ICC codes (as well as the last editions of the legacy codes) use the Common Code Format. The NFPA uses the Manual of Style.

10. *Americans with Disabilities Act Accessibility Guidelines*

11. occupancy (or occupancy classification)

12. Access Board (or ATBCB)

13. The various states include: Arkansas, California, Florida, Georgia, Louisiana, Massachusetts, Michigan, Minnesota, New Jersey, New York, North Carolina, Ohio, Oregon, Virginia.
    The various cities include: Boston, Dallas, Houston, and Los Angeles.

14. Underwriter Laboratories (or UL)

15. c. Although the NFPA may cover these topics in other code documents such as the *NFPA 5000* and *Life Safety Code*, they do not have separate publications for these items.

16. b. Although a team approach is recommended, it may not always be required. If it is required, the team leader can vary but typically needs to be a licensed design professional. Most often it will be an architect or an engineer.

17. a. The code documents that you need to reference depend on what is required and/or allowed by the jurisdiction, not the type of the project.

18. e. The ADA has four title sections. It regulates employment, public accommodations (including commercial facilities), telecommunications, and transportation. It does not regulate federal buildings or one and two family dwellings.

19. b. The ADA is federal law; the *ADAAG* is a set of guidelines to follow in order to meet the minimum requirements of the ADA. It deals primarily with Title III of the ADA.

20. d. There is no such thing as the American Standards Act.

21. a. American National Standards Institute (or ASTM International).

22. e. All of these deal with accessibility issues. (The *UFAS* is the *Uniform Federal Accessibility Standards*.)

23. b. Selecting the strictest (or most restrictive) code requirement will usually work, even if you have to select from a range of dimensions. For example, if the codes require handrails at 30–38 inches and an accessibility regulation allows 34–38 inches, the accessibility regulation is the most restrictive. It will satisfy both requirements.

24. b. Always ask the code official (or code department) located in the jurisdiction of the project.

CHAPTER 2. Occupancy Classifications and Loads

1. **True.** The occupancy classification is needed to determine most of the other code requirements. (It should be determined in conjunction with occupant load.)

2. **False.** The smaller occupancy would only be considered accessory if it is less than 10 percent of the total area of the two spaces.

3. **False.** It depends on the size. If more than 100 square feet (9.3 s m) the storage room is typically considered an incidental use, and would only be treated as part of the predominate occupancy if the appropriate fire protection is provided.

4. **True.** If the required fire-resistance-rated walls are not properly located in a building with more than one occupancy, the requirements of the most restrictive occupancy will usually apply to all occupancies in the building.

5. Can include: Detentional/Correctional (or Restrained), Health Care (or Unrestrained), Day Care, or Residential Board and Care

6. risk factors

7. gross

8. physical and health

9. f. Supermarket (Mercantile occupancy)
g. Refinery (Industrial occupancy)
b. Gas plant (Hazardous occupancy)
c. Bank (Business occupancy)
a. Nursing home (Institutional occupancy)
h. Kindergarten (Educational occupancy)
i. Dormitory (Residential occupancy)
d. Church (Assembly occupancy)
e. Freight terminal (Storage occupancy)

10. c. Number of occupants is especially important in certain subclassifications of occupancies such as Institutional and Residential (as well as Assembly in the NFPA codes). Unusual hazards and certain

types of activities can also change the occupancy classification. The size of the building does not matter, since there may be more than one occupancy classification inside the building. Although the rating of walls is important, they do not determine the occupancy classification. (Note that the building type or use of the space is also required to determine the occupancy classification.)

11. e. Although changing the number of employees can sometimes affect the subclassification of the occupancy, it does not usually affect the occupancy itself. For example, in a Business occupancy, a fluctuating number of employees will not change the occupancy type. (Note that in Residential and Institutional occupancies, the staff is usually not counted in the number of employees.)

12. d. In the *International Building Code*, Assembly subclassifications are based on the type of activity, not the number of occupants. (The NFPA, on the other hand, does use the number of occupants to determine the Assembly subclassification.) Educational occupancies are based on the age of the occupant and length of stay.

13. a. College classrooms are usually classified as a Business occupancy. If the classroom is a larger (lecture hall type) room, it may be classified as an Assembly occupancy.

14. c. Although a nursing home can be considered Residential if there is a small number of occupants, it is generally considered an Institutional or Health Care occupancy.

15. a. Depending on the building code, a restaurant is usually considered a Business or an Assembly occupancy. Each of the other building types will usually consist of more than one occupancy classification.

16. c. Institutional, Business, and Mercantile occupancies are typically considered public accommodations. The original ADA guidelines includes special sections to cover Assembly, Business, Mercantile, Institutional, and Residential (transient) occupancies. (Similar information is included in the new guidelines.) Although Factories would be covered by the ADA as a commercial facility, the ADA guidelines does not provide specific requirements for this occupancy.

17. b. The 10 percent requirement pertains to 10 percent of the entire space (including the accessory use), not just the area of the primary occupancy.

18. e. By definition, mixed multiple occupancies in the NFPA and non-separated mixed occupancies in the ICC are not considered separate from each other so the most stringent requirements will apply.

19. d. Although increasing the occupant load can affect the rating of some walls, such as exit access corridors, it would not require *all* interior walls to be rated.

20. e. The occupant load is typically required to determine means of egress requirements and plumbing fixture quantities. Jurisdictions may also use the occupancy load to determine the maximum number of people allowed to occupy the space at a given time, especially in Assembly occupancies.

21. d. Based on the formula, the occupant load is determined by dividing the floor area by the load factor.

22. d. The occupant load for each occupancy is determined separately and added together.

23. a. Since the load factor can vary based on the building type and use of the space, you may need to do more than one calculation to determine which use will allow the largest number of people.

24. e. Fixed seating most often includes benches, bleachers, pews, and booth seating. However, rows of chairs that are rarely moved (i.e., ganged stacking chairs) could also be considered fixed seating.

CHAPTER 3. Construction Types and Building Sizes

1. **False.** Interior walls do not typically affect the construction type. This can be seen in Figure 3.1 of the *Guidebook*. (Some of the legacy codes did include rating requirements for certain interior walls as part of their construction types, but the newer codes do not.)

2. **True.** In the ICC and NFPA codes, construction types range from Type I, the strictest, to Type V.

3. **True.**

4. **False.** All buildings are classified with a construction type and must maintain the fire-resistance ratings of the construction type as defined by the building code at the time it was constructed.

5. **True.**

6. resistant

7. building (shaft enclosures are not structural elements)

8. heavy timber

9. c. Some amounts and types of combustible materials are allowed in every construction type. Examples include wood blocking and furring strips. (Also see the inset titled *Use of Combustible Materials* on page 199 of the *Guidebook*.)

10. c. Type I and II primarily use noncombustible materials throughout, Type IV consists primarily of heavy timber, and Type V typically uses combustible materials (i.e., wood) for exterior and interior elements.

11. b. Chemically treated wood, also known as FRTW, is actually known as *fire retardant* treated wood.

12. a. A fire retardant only delays a combustible material from being consumed by a fire. It will eventually contribute to the fuel of a fire.

13. e. A party wall and a fire wall are the same thing. They can be used to create what is considered two or more buildings. A parapet is only the top portion of a fire wall.

14. a. Assembly because of the quantity of occupants, and Institutional because of the restricted mobility of its occupants. (Hazardous occupancies also typically require stricter construction types.)

15. e. The construction type of a building and the use of an automatic sprinkler system can affect the allowable square footage (square meter) or area of a building. However, all three factors need to be known in order to determine if a specific building or space is suitable for a certain use or occupancy type.

16. e.

17. c. Changing the construction type helps only if it gets stricter. A tenant separation wall does not help, although a fire wall could make a difference.

CHAPTER 4. Means of Egress

1. **False.** A means of egress must be an unobstructed path that leads a person either safely out of a building or into an area of refuge. The pathway must meet certain code requirements. For example, although escalators and elevators are often used as part of the general circulation within a building, the codes generally do not allow them to be a means of egress unless very specific code requirements are met (i.e., escalators must be fully enclosed by rated assemblies and elevator shafts must meet requirements for smoke and fire protection).

2. **False.** All doors must swing into the stairway except at ground level. This door must swing out toward the exit discharge or exterior of the building.

3. **False.** It is the opposite. They must be 10 feet (3048 mm) wide or more to be considered a public way.

4. **True.** There may be some other ways to describe them; however, this is the main difference between the two.

5. **False.** The doorway can be larger than 48 inches (1220 mm) wide. It is the leaf of the door that cannot be more than 48 inches (1220 mm) wide.

6. **True.** (Note that floors below ground level may have different requirements.)

7. public way (or area of refuge—see answer #15)

8. The most common answers would include: lever, push-type, panic bar, and U-shaped.

9. 12 feet (or 3660 mm)

10. The most common answers would include no exit, stair number, floor number, keep door closed, and area of refuge.

11. passageway. It is an example of a type of exit discharge.

12. remotely. The first two exits must follow the half diagonal rule.

13. exit

14. d. The allowed fire (and smoke) ratings of walls and other assemblies as well as allowed finishes are based on the type of means of egress. Occupant load is used to determine the means of egress.

15. b. An *area of refuge* can also be the final destination either when used in conjunction with a stairwell or when using a horizontal exit.

16. a.

17. b. Exits always need to be fully enclosed; exit accesses do not. *Exit access stairs* are sometimes allowed to be open when they connect two floors within the same tenant space. *Intervening rooms* such as reception areas are not always fully enclosed.

18. a. 90 inches (2286 mm) is the required ceiling height but some items are allowed to project down from the ceiling up to 10 inches (254 mm) for a minimum head clearance of 80 inches (2032 mm).

19. b. A corridor can be used in a means of egress in three ways. A corridor used as an exit is called an exit passageway. (A corridor used as an exit access is called an exit access corridor. A corridor used as an exit discharge is called a discharge corridor.)

20. b.

21. a. The codes allow exceptions to the door swinging in the direction of exit travel, especially in smaller occupancies or rooms.

22. b. 7 inches (180 mm) is typically the maximum dimension, not the minimum; the maximum nosing projection is 1½ inches (38 mm); and the codes allow some exceptions to stairs with handrails on both sides (especially in some Residential occupancies).

23. a. Especially hospitals and prisons. Others would include Storage and Industrial occupancies (and high-rise buildings).

24. c. File/storage rooms are more likely to be locked. They may also contain hazardous contents.

25. a. If required, the area of refuge must be located adjacent to the elevator shaft (similar to Plan C in Figure 4.12 as shown in the *Guidebook*), not anywhere on the floor.

26. d. A sprinkler system is not required. In fact, if the building has an approved sprinkler system, an area of refuse may not be required.

27. b. You must calculate each tenant or occupant load separately and add them together to determine the number of exits for a whole floor.

28. c. 44 inches (1118 mm) is the typical minimum building code corridor width. 36 inches (815 mm) is allowed in some Residential occupancies and is the typical minimum accessible corridor width.

29. e. All are allowed exceptions.

30. d.

31. b. Longer lengths are usually allowed in buildings equipped with an automatic sprinkler system.

32. d. The location of an exit is typically determined by the half diagonal rule.

33. b. The width of an exit in a means of egress should never be reduced as it travels toward the exit discharge.

34. c. In determining the required width, the codes require that an additional 19 inches (483 mm), not 18 inches (445 mm), be added to the code minimum or required calculation.

□ CHAPTER 5. Fire-Resistant Materials and Assemblies

1. **False.** A *passive* fire protection system is what is sometimes referred to as a prevention system.

2. **False.** The fire-resistance rating can also be controlled by the walls that surround the floor/ceiling assembly. For example, some occupancy classifications require certain rooms (such as a mechanical or boiler room) to be surrounded by fire barriers. This would include the walls as well as the floor/ceiling assemblies above and below within these rooms.

3. **False.** Most fire-protection rated doors must have a closing device, but it does not necessarily have to be automatic closing. A self-closing device can also be used. A self-closing device, such as a door closer, will close the door after each use. An automatic-closing device is usually activated by an alarm so that it closes a door that is typically used in the open position.

4. **True.** For example, a rated door can be considered a through-penetration and typically has a lower rating than the rated wall in which it is located.

5. **False.** Smokestop doors are specially designed to inhibit the passage of smoke and must pass additional testing.

6. **True.**

7. **False.** Although they are similar, occupancy separation walls separate different occupancies within the same building. A demising wall, which is another name for a tenant separation wall, separates different tenants of the same occupancy type. These walls typically have different ratings and requirements.

8. **False.** Most fire-protection rated doors are allowed to have glass lites. However, the codes specify the type of glass that can be used and limit the size of the glass.

9. Fire (or party)

10. hardware (or sill, or doorway)

11. enclosure

12. a. *Installation of Smoke Door Assemblies (NFPA 105)*
    e. *Fire Doors and Fire Windows (NFPA 80)*
    f. *Fire Test for Window and Glass Block Assemblies (NFPA 257)*
    b. *Fire Test of Door Assemblies (NFPA 252)*
    d. *Tests of Fire Endurance of Building Construction and Materials (NFPA 251)*
    c. *Fire Walls and Fire Barrier Walls (NFPA 221)*

13. c. A tenant separation wall is also known as a demising wall and is used between tenant spaces, dwelling units, or sleeping rooms.

14. a. Fireblocks and draftstops are used in concealed spaces. Firestops have two ratings; however the T-rating is stricter. (It includes the F-rating plus an additional maximum temperature rise requirement.)

15. d. Common examples include an exit stair that serves more than four stories, a horizontal exit, and an exit passageway. Exit discharges are typically allowed to have lower fire ratings than exits.

16. b. Fireblocking is used in small, concealed spaces. Firestops and dampers are used at openings in rated assemblies.

17. e.

18. a. It can be required in both a separated mixed occupancy according to the *IBC* and in a separated multiple occupancy according to the NFPA codes.

19. d. Tempered glass is typically not rated. Only if it is specially treated can it receive a 20-minute rating.

20. e. All fully enclosed smoke barriers require additional ventilation and air circulation.

21. c. Hinges must be steel or stainless steel. Most sills must be accessible, especially when used in a means of egress and other accessible paths. Currently, the codes provide sizes only for wire glass in rated doors.

22. e. All are common examples of fire partitions required by the *IBC*.

23. c.

24. d. Smoke barriers prevent the movement of smoke. Pressurized exits prevent smoke from following escaping occupants. Sprinklers concentrate on controlling a fire.

25. b. Ceiling dampers are used at a duct or diffuser located in a suspended ceiling to prevent heat from entering the space between the suspended ceiling and the rated floor assembly above.

26. c. Smoke dampers are typically used inside the duct.

27. d. An electrical box can compromise the rating of a rated wall, but only if it is not installed properly.

28. c.

☐CHAPTER 6. Fire Protection Systems

1. **False.** Both multiple and single station smoke detectors must be tied into the building's power source.

2. **False.** Although budget may be a consideration, the choice of system will most often be dictated by the codes based on the occupancy type.

3. **False.** New technology (i.e., building automation systems) allows fire and smoke alarm systems to be tied to other building controls such as the mechanical system or the security system, although some jurisdictions may restrict the extent of these connections.

4. **False.** Depending on the type of detector, a detection system can detect smoke and other gases, heat and other changes in temperature, or multiple symptoms of fire.

5. **True.** An alarm system can be activated manually using a pull station or automatically upon the operation of an automatic sprinkler system, fire detection system, or smoke detection system.

6. **True.** (See Figure 6.2 in *Guidebook*.)

7. **False.** Fire extinguishers can be surface mounted using a bracket or recessed within a wall using a cabinet. The cabinet can either have a vision panel or have a solid door that is clearly marked.

8. visual

9. 75 feet (or 22,860 mm)

10. d. *Portable Fire Extinguishers (NFPA 10)*
    e. *National Fire Alarm Code (NFPA 72)*

a. *National Electrical Code (NFPA 70)*
f. *Installation of Sprinkler Systems (NFPA 13)*
b. *Emergency and Standby Power Systems (NFPA 110)*
g. *Fire Safety Symbols (NFPA 170)*
c. *Carbon Dioxide Extinguishing Systems (NFPA 12)*

11. d. Voice communication systems use an intercom to verbally direct the occupants out of a building. Emergency alarm systems usually include a voice communication system. An accessible warning system encompasses devises that would be used in addition to typical visual, audio and voice communication systems (i.e., tactile notification, text messaging, etc.).

12. e.

13. d. A firestop is a through-penetration protective and part of a prevention system. A manual fire alarm is part of the detection system because it is a device activated by an occupant upon detection of a fire.

14. b. A manual alarm system is considered a detection system because occupants can use it after they detect a fire.

15. d. Emergency alarm systems are most often required in high-rise buildings as well as hazardous building types such as factories and large storage facilities.

16. b. Class III is also designed for occupant use, but that is not its primary function. It is equipped with an outlet for fire department use, as well. Class I is primarily for fire department use.

17. b. Although usually located in stairwells, the quantity of stairs does not determine if a standpipe is required.

18. e.

19. b. In a dry pipe system the pipes are filled with pressurized air or nitrogen until the heat from a fire causes the pipes to fill with water.

20. a. When an automatic sprinkler system is provided in a building, the codes allow a variety of trade-offs, but sprinklers do not affect the occupancy classification of a building or space. (See Figure 6.6 in the *Guidebook* for additional allowances or trade-offs.)

21. b. Sprinkler head types include standard, fast-response, residential, quick-response, extended coverage, large drop, open as well as other specialty types.

22. b. This is typical, although specialty sprinklers may require additional clearances.

23. e. There are alarm and accessible warning system requirements, as well as a few general accessible requirements such as reaching distances and protrusions into the path of travel.

24. a. The codes often limit the use of sprinklers in restaurant kitchens due to the amount of heat that is naturally created and the possibility of grease fires. Instead, sprinklers are usually required only in kitchen exhaust systems.

25. a.

☐ CHAPTER 7. Plumbing and Mechanical Requirements

1. **True.** This is especially true in the I-Codes since the *IBC* includes the table for plumbing fixtures as well as other facility requirements. The building codes also typically include requirements for plumbing related items such as standpipes, fire hoses, and sprinkler systems.

2. **True.** Generally, every floor will require a minimum of *one* toilet or restroom per gender—one male and one female. In some cases these can be combined into a single unisex toilet facility when the occupant load is limited.

3. **False.** It is the other way around. There are usually more water closets than lavatories.

4. **True.** They need to be planned at the same time because these systems often overlap each other in a building. In addition, they can affect a number of other building elements, such as the height of a suspended ceiling.

5. **False.** Not only are some of the requirements found in the building codes (including the environmental chapters) and the energy codes, but there are also a number of standards, such as those from ANSI and ASHRAE.

6. **True.**

7. contractor

8. nonabsorbent

9. water closet

10. 6.5 inches (or 165 mm)

11. ventilation

12. load

13. e. In addition to all plumbing fixtures, sprinklers, standpipes, fire hoses, and fire extinguishers are also considered part of a building's plumbing system.

14. a. You need to determine the occupancy classification of a project before you can determine the occupant load. The occupant load is then used with the code tables to determine the quantity and type of fixtures.

15. c. A toilet in a tenant space cannot be deducted from the total common facilities required for that floor, since it is not available for everyone on the floor to use.

16. b. Although facilities must be available to employees and customers, they do not need to be separate. The facilities must typically be located in employee areas unless they are not accessible to the public.

17. c. A unisex toilet may be required when 6 or more water closets are provided, not 8.

18. d. The plumbing codes specify the finish requirements of a plumbing fixture.

19. c. Some accessibility codes may allow between 16 and 18 inches (405 and 455 mm), but 18 inches (455 mm) is most universal. 15 inches (381 mm) is what is required by codes for nonaccessible water closets.

20. a. They are most commonly used in schools, restaurants, clubs, lounges, transportation terminals, auditoriums, theaters, and churches. All of these can be classified as an Assembly or an Educational occupancy.

21. d. It depends on the location of the drinking fountain. If it is not located in a corridor or protruding into a path of accessible travel it does not need to meet this accessibility requirement.

22. b.

23. c. The codes require water closets to have an elongated bowl with a seat open at the front. Bathtubs are typically required only in Residential occupancies. The swing of a door will affect length and/or depth of an accessible toilet stall. And, accessible sinks and lavatories have similar knee and toe clearance requirements.

24. b. A drinking fountain can be installed in the corridor leading to a toilet facility, but the codes do not allow one in the vestibule leading into the toilet facility. Laminate is considered impervious material and therefore can be used on toilet stalls. All toilet accessories can be mounted at the same accessible height, even though only a percentage are required to be accessible.

25. c. Although water closets and bathing fixtures require a variety of clear floor space sizes, 30 by 48 inches (760 by 1220 mm) is required at almost all other accessible fixtures and at all accessible accessories.

26. d. Residential occupancies include dormitories, hotels, and apartments. Assembly occupancies include gymnasiums and health clubs. Institutional occupancies include hospitals, prisons, and nursing homes.

(Although dormitories and gymnasiums may be located in an educational facility, they are often considered a separate occupancy. Only certain Industrial occupancies require shower facilities.)

27. b. A curb at an accessible shower can be as high as 0.5 inches (13 mm). However, if it is more than 0.25 inches (6.4 mm) high, the edges must be beveled.

28. e. It is appropriate to use the symbol in all these locations. However, in new buildings it is common not to show the symbol on any of the restroom signs because all restrooms should be accessible. A building with a nonaccessible restroom must include the symbol on the sign to indicate the location to the nearest accessible facility.

29. d. Suspended ceilings create a horizontal ceiling plenum. A shaft plenum would be vertical.

30. e.

31. b. Ducts are still needed in plenum air systems, but only to supply the air to the space. The ceiling plenum collects the air without return ducts.

32. a. The office would most likely be grouped together with the other interior offices into one zone. (If it was a larger executive office, it may be given its own thermostat.)

33. e. A code jurisdiction may add an amendment to the mechanical code publication requiring an engineer, even though the original text does not require it.

34. e. A plumbing system also affects energy consumption. When less water is used, less energy is needed by the utility company and by the building to heat and/or distribute the water.

☐ CHAPTER 8. Electrical and Communication Requirements

1. **True.** The *NEC* does not typically regulate public services. It is the ADA that regulates public phones for accessibility.

2. **True.**

3. **False.** They are also installed in ceilings for light fixtures.

4. **False.** They are similar, but not the same. Both are used to supply power when the normal power source fails. However, an *emergency electrical system* is for operating emergency systems, such as exit signs and automatic door locks, and a *standby power system* is used for less critical building systems, such as general lighting and elevators.

5. **False.** Although required in sleeping rooms, AFCI requirements apply to all electrical outlets in the room, including wall, floor and ceiling outlets as well as light fixtures and smoke detectors.

6. **True.**

7. ground

8. 6 feet (or 1.8 meter). This is typically accomplished by placing an outlet every 12 feet (3656 mm) along a wall. (Note that in commercial applications, receptacles are typically placed for convenience.)

9. 10 seconds

10. voltage(s)

11. b. *NFPA 70* is the same thing as the *National Electrical Code.*

12. a. The designer will typically locate the outlets and select some or all of the light fixtures. The engineer will design the corresponding electrical system and confirm that everything meets the electrical codes.

13. e. All are tied into the electrical system of a building.

14. a. The branch panelboards supply electricity to different areas on the same floor. The switchboard is the main panel that connects to the utility service. (There is no such thing as a branch switchboard.)

15. a. Flex cable is the same thing as BX cable, which is often used on 2 × 4 suspended light fixtures.

16. d.

17. c. It is typically prohibited in residential, hospital, and school buildings. The *NEC* also prohibits the use of flat wire in wet and other hazardous areas.

18. a. Romex cables are typically limited to one- and two-family dwellings and multi-unit dwellings.

19. b. This is the lowest reaching height allowed for a person in a wheelchair.

20. b. Even though only UL-approved (or labeled) light fixtures can be used on the interior of a building, the light fixture must be specially rated to be allowed in fire-resistance rated ceilings.

21. d. In dwelling unit kitchens typically only the outlets located near cabinetry or the wet area must be GFCI. However, in commercial restrooms and kitchens (including breakrooms) typically all outlets in the room must be GFCI.

22. b. This code requirement applies to electrical boxes, as well as wires, cables, and conduit.

23. e.

24. a. Conduit is also available in plastic but this is typically allowed only in nonrated applications.

25. c. A junction box is a generic electrical box where wires can be terminated for future use, spliced together to add additional devices, and so on. It allows access to these wires.

26. a. Hanging (or pendant) light fixtures are allowed, but they must be mounted so that they are located outside the restricted area around the tub or shower. (See Figure 8.7 in the *Guidebook*.)

27. e.

28. a.

29. f. Although in the past, a communication system consisted primarily of a telephone system, it now can include computer data, security, cable, and satellite services, among others.

30. d. Similar to electrical closets, communication and satellite closets usually do not need to meet requirements as stringent as the main telecommunication room.

31. e. Fiber optic cables
    d. Twisted pair cables
    b. Wireless
    f. Zone cabling
    a. Coaxial cables
    c. Composite cables

32. c. Cable trays are not the only method to neatly run cables in a ceiling. Only abandoned cables that are accessible (i.e., easily reached) need to be removed. Although electrical and communication outlets are usually mounted adjacent to each other, the cables are not typically allowed to share the same conduit.

☐ CHAPTER 9. Finish and Furniture Selection

1. **True.**

2. **False.** They are both *Pill Tests* (also known as *Methenamine Pill Tests*).

3. **False.** To pass the *CAL 133* test, a piece of furniture must be tested as a *whole*. That means setting the sofa on fire, which would ruin it.

4. **False.** The thermally thin requirement in the codes is limited to finishes applied to *noncombustible* surfaces, such as gypsum board, plaster, brick, or concrete.

5. **True**. Required finish classes become stricter as you move from an interior room to an exit access corridor to an exit stair, so that as the occupants move away from the flames, the way to safety is free of fire and smoke.

6. **False**. If a finish is not tested, it may be possible to treated it to obtain the appropriate rating.

7. block (or blocker)

8. Flashover

9. treatment

10. worksurfaces (or tables)

11. b. *Pill Test (DOC FF1-70)*
    h. *Steiner Tunnel Test (ASTM E84)*
    e. *Vertical Flame Test (NFPA 701)*
    c. *Radiant Panel Test (ASTM E648)*
    a. *Room Corner Test (NFPA 265)*
    f. *Toxicity Test (NFPA 269)*
    d. *Smolder Resistance Test (NFPA 260)*
    g. *Mattress Test (DOC FF4-72)*

12. b.

13. c. This test is required in building types such as hospitals and jails as well as Residential occupancies such as hotels and dormitories. (*DOC FF4-72* is also a mattress test, but it is required on most mattresses sold and used in the United States.)

14. c. Also known as the *Flooring Radiant Panel Test,* it is primarily used for rating interior floor finishes.

15. e. The *Pitts Test* is a toxicity test, which is used to test a wide variety of finishes, furnishings, and building materials.

16. a. Although certain occupancies may typically have different building sizes than others, it is the occupancy classification, not the building size, that matters. The location of a finish, especially in a means of egress, makes a difference, as well. The jurisdiction also affects what is required, both by mandating a specific code publication and by amending the code to require additional finish and furniture tests.

17. c. The 2003 edition of the *Life Safety Code* now references the ASTM version, but not all jurisdictions use the *LSC*. Some jurisdictions have passed the legislation necessary to enforce *CAL 133* and others may do so in the future.

18. d.

19. e.

20. a. The *Room Corner Test* is specifically used when napped, tufted, or looped textiles and carpets are used on walls and ceilings.

21. d. All Smolder Resistance Tests use a cigarette and measure a char mark.

22. b. The *Steiner Tunnel Test* measures the flame spread (or FSI) and smoke development (or SDI).

23. d. These types of finishes include draperies and wall hangings, among other things.

24. e. Often, the treatment company will be able to tell from the content of the fabric how it will react to a treatment. However, having a fabric sample tested is the only way to know for sure.

25. d. These include occupancies that have evacuation restrictions and overnight provisions. Building types such as hospitals, prisons, and hotels tend to be the strictest.

26. a. In buildings that require rated finishes and furniture, the use of an automatic sprinkler system will often allow finishes with lower ratings to be used. Rarely will the use of sprinklers eliminate the need for rated finishes.

27. e. If any of these finishes cover 10 percent or less of a wall area or ceiling, they are usually allowed to have a lower finish rating. Nontested finishes may also be allowed.

28. a. Exits typically require higher finish ratings than exit accesses and other interior spaces.

29. b.

30. d. There cannot be a drastic level change between two different types of flooring. Marble floors tend to be thicker than carpet. The marble subfloor typically needs to be recessed so that the top of the marble and carpet will align. Although a carpet pad can create a problem for wheelchair use, thin double stick pads usually do not.

31. b. Although the test samples in *Smolder Resistant Tests* may include fabrics and foams, the tests were developed specifically for a full mock-up of a piece of furniture rather than individual items.

32. a. The symbols are used primarily on textiles and are not used on furniture.

33. a. You should be keeping abreast of the newest finish and furniture code requirements and most advanced industry standards used throughout the country (and in other countries), not just within your jurisdiction. When allowed by the jurisdiction, you may want to use more restrictive finish standards to provide additional safety. Certain federal regulations may also apply. Keep a record of your research and why you used certain standards over others.

CHAPTER 10. Code Officials and the Code Process

1. **False.** Projects that require minimal finish and furniture installation will typically not need a permit. Other smaller interior projects, in smaller buildings or residential houses, may not need a permit either, depending on the jurisdiction.

2. **True.** Because codes typically indicate the final result that must be obtained, there is often more than one way to accomplish that result.

3. **False.** The Board cannot waive a code. It can only decide if the appeal meets the interpretation of the code.

4. **False.** Although some federal agencies do have formal reviews available, this is a lengthy process and should only be reserved for very large or public projects. Rather, you should be familiar enough with federal requirements to include the necessary information in your drawings.

5. department, official

6. permit

7. programming. Although code research will continue throughout the design phases, you should start as soon as possible.

8. contractor (or subcontractor)

9. specifications

10. d. The drawings are reviewed by the plans examiner for code and standards compliance and by the fire marshal for fire code compliance. (In some jurisdictions this may be one and the same person.) The building inspector checks for compliance in the field during construction.

11. b. The correct code jurisdiction must be determined before you know which codes department to contact to answer the remaining questions.

12. b. Obtaining a permit is typically done by a contractor or subcontractor.

13. c. Permits are typically required when construction or alterations are made to a building, when there is a change in occupancy, and/or when regulated equipment is installed. Projects that require only finish and furniture installation will typically not need a permit.

14. c. During the schematic phase, you will have enough drawings done to have them reviewed. If changes need to be made, it is less costly to do them at this point rather than in the construction drawing phase.

15. e. Cost alone should not be a reason to go through the appeals process. However, if the related cost is disproportionate to the overall cost of the project and there is a viable alternate solution available, it is more likely an appeal will be granted.

16. c. An appeal (or variance) can be used only on the project in question. All projects requiring a permit must go through the permit review process. Some jurisdictions do not always require stamped construction documents, especially for projects in smaller buildings.

17. b. A footing inspection is typically required in new construction and is part of the foundation of a building.

18. e. Although the inspector's main job is to make sure the construction meets code, he or she also checks the construction documents to make sure what was approved during plan review is being done. The codes department issues a Certificate of Occupancy after the final inspection.

19. a. Performance codes should not be used to avoid building something just for cost reasons.

20. b. A code department is not required to have the documentation reviewed by an outside consultant. It will be depend on the extent of the project, the type of performance criteria used, the format of the documentation, and the expertise of the code official(s).

SECTION 5

ANSWERS TO STUDY PROBLEMS

☐ CHAPTER 1. About the Codes

PROBLEM 1

Code Organizations:
  1. International Code Council (ICC)
  2. National Fire Protection Association (NFPA)

Standards Organizations:
  1. National Fire Protection Association (NFPA)
  2. American National Standards Institute (ANSI)
  3. American Society for Testing and Materials (ASTM or ASTM International)
  4. American Society of Heating, Refrigeration, and Air conditioning Engineers (ASHRAE)
  5. Underwriters Laboratories (UL)

Federal Departments:
  1. Architectural and Transportation Barriers Compliance Board (or Access Board) (ATCBC)
  2. Department of Housing and Urban Development (HUD)
  3. Department of Justice (DOJ)

PROBLEM 2

  ABA—*Architectural Barriers Act*
  ADA—*Americans with Disabilities Act*
  FHA—*Fair Housing Act*
  IBC—*International Building Code*
  ICC/ANSI—*ICC/ANSI A117.14 Standard on Accessible and Useable Building and Facilities*
  ICCEC—*ICC Electrical Code–Administrative Provisions*
  ICCPC—*International Code Council Performance Code*
  IEBC—*International Existing Building Code*
  IECC—*International Energy Conservation Code*
  IFC—*International Fire Code*
  IMC—*International Mechanical Code*
  IPC—*International Plumbing Code*
  IRC—*International Residential Code*
  LSC—*Life Safety Code* (or *NFPA 101*)
  NEC—*National Electrical Code* (or *NFPA 70*)
  UFAS—*Uniform Federal Accessibility Standards*
  UFC—*Uniform Fire Code* (or *NFPA 1*)
  UMC —*Uniform Mechanical Code*
  UPC—*Uniform Plumbing Code*

CHAPTER 2. Occupancy Classifications and Loads

PROBLEM 1

a. Institutional, Restrained (or I-3).
   Explanation: Prisons are considered Institutional occupancies. Of the four subclassifications listed, I-3 describes a prison best.

b. Residential, Hotels and Dormitories (or R-A).
   Explanation: Although hotels are considered a type of Residential occupancy, the NFPA codes have a specific subclassification for Hotels. So, when using the *NFPA 5000*, you would refer to the requirements for a Hotel occupancy.

c. The expected number of occupants (i.e., employees and patrons)?
   Explanation: Although a nightclub is clearly an Assembly occupancy, the NFPA codes further subdivide Assembly occupancies based on the occupant load. Thus, you need to know whether the occupant load will be 50–300, 300–1000 or more than 1000. Each subclassification may have different requirements for finishes.

d. Assembly (or A-2), because of the consumption of food and drink.
   Explanation: The *IBC* defines Assembly uses by the specific type of activity such as serving food and drink, not by the number of people in the space as does the NFPA codes. So, in this case, the occupant load does not matter. (In some cases, when using the NFPA codes and some legacy codes, however, if the number of occupants is less than 50 or 100, a restaurant could be reclassified as a Business occupancy.)

e. Assembly (A-C), because this assembly subclassification is for occupant loads between or equal to 50 and 300. The restaurant falls in this range.

PROBLEM 2

Occupant load of Figure 2.1 = 52.

Explanation: The occupant load is determined by calculating the square footage (or square meters) of the space and dividing it by the occupant load factors found in the *IBC* Table 1004.1.2. You were told the space is a retail store. This is a Mercantile occupancy. Looking on the table under "Occupancy," there are three categories under "Mercantile." Since you were told that this store is on the ground floor, you will use the second category, "Basement and grade floor areas." This allows you 30 gross square feet (2.8 s m) of area per occupant. Notice, however, that there is also a category called "Storage, stock, and shipping area." If you look at the floor plan, it shows that the rear of the store will be used for storage. This area will be calculated separately using 300 gross square feet (28 s m) per occupant. (Both categories require gross area so include all miscellaneous spaces in your calculations.)

Since there are two different load factors, two square footage calculations must be made. Using the formula *Occupant Load = Floor Area ÷ Load Factor,* the occupant load is determined as follows:

SPACE	LOAD FACTOR	SIZE OF SPACE	FLOOR AREA	OCCUPANT LOAD
Retail Area	30 gross (2.787 s m)	48.5 × 31 (14.78 × 9.45)	1503.5 sf (139.7 s m)	1503.5 ÷ 30 = 50.12 (139.7 ÷ 2.787 = 50.12)
Storage Area	300 gross (27.87 s m)	14 × 31 (4.27 × 9.45)	434 (40.35 s m)	434 ÷ 300 = 1.45 (40.35 ÷ 27.87 = 1.45)

Using the calculations for feet and inches, the total occupant load is 50.12 for the retail area, plus 1.45 for the storage area. This equals 51.57, which rounds up to 52. (*Note:* The codes indicate that you should always round up when a total results in a fraction.)

PROBLEM 3

a. Plan B; because the Storage occupancy is less than 10 percent of the entire building and it is too large to be considered an incidental room.

Explanation: The storage area in Plan A is small enough to be considered a room within a larger use, but not a separate use. This room would be considered an "incidental use" but not an accessory use.

The storage area in Plan C could not be considered an accessory use, either. To be considered an accessory use by the codes, the storage area must be less than 10 percent of the total area. If you add the two spaces together, the total area of the building is 6000 (557.4 s m). To be considered an accessory use, the Storage use would have to be less than 10 percent of 6000 square feet (557.4 s m) or 600 square feet (55.7 s m). (Instead, it would be considered a separate occupancy classification from the A-2 and be considered a mixed occupancy.)

In the case of Plan D, the Storage use is larger than the Factory use and thus cannot be considered an accessory use. (This would also be considered a mixed occupancy building.)

b. Occupant load of Figure 2.2A = 250.

Explanation: The occupant load is determined by calculating the square footage (or square meters) of the space and dividing it by the occupant load factors found in the *IBC* Table 1004.1.2 for each type of use. To determine the occupant load for the entire building, you must first calculate the occupant load of each occupancy type or use and then add together. First, start by calculating the occupant load of the Educational (E) area. To do this, you divide the area of the Educational portion of the building by the floor area factor found in the *IBC* table. The area of the Educational part of the building is shown on the Plan A to be 5000 square feet (464.5 s m). In Table 1004.1.2, you can see that the Educational use has two separate load factors. Since you were told that the Educational use was primarily classrooms, you will use the load factor given for "Classroom area" which is 20 net square feet (1.858 s m) per occupant.

Occupant load = Floor area ÷ Load factor

Occupant load = 5000 NSF ÷ 20 NSF = 250 occupants

or

Occupant load = 464.5 NSM ÷ 1.858 NSM = 250 occupants

Now consider the area of the Storage use. Because the Storage area was determined in the previous question to be an incidental room, it is considered to be a part of the Educational use. Notice that the load factor used to determine the occupant load of the Educational area requires a net area. From what you know about the code you remember that net areas do not include utility or nonoccupied spaces. So the area of the Storage incidental room is not calculated and will not be counted toward the total occupant load of the building. The total occupant load for the building remains at 250 occupants.

PROBLEM 4

Occupant load of Figure 2.3 = 186.

Explanation: This situation is an example of having to combine the occupant loads of primary and secondary spaces in order to determine the total occupant load. So, in order to determine the occupant load of the central Student Lounge area, you must first calculate the occupant load for that specific space and then add the number of occupants from the adjacent areas that must pass through the Student Lounge on their way to the final exit.

First, determine the occupant load for the Student Lounge for its specific use. As a gathering space, it is considered an Assembly. You have been told that this area is primarily used with tables and chairs. So, referring to the *IBC* Table 1004.1.2, you would use the load factor for "Assembly, Unconcentrated (tables and chairs)" which is 15 net square feet (1.39 s m). You also need to determine the size of the Student Lounge. Using the dimensions on the floor plan you can tell that the space is 20 feet (6.1 m) wide by 50 feet (15.2 m) long. If you multiply these, the total area equals 1000 square feet (92.9 s m). (Restrooms would not be included since you are using a "net" load factor.)

$$\text{Occupant load} = \text{Floor area} \div \text{Load factor}$$

$$\text{Occupant load} = 1000 \text{ NSF} \div 15 \text{ NSF} = 66.7 \text{ or } 67 \text{ occupants}$$

or

$$\text{Occupant load} = 92.9 \text{ NSM} \div 1.39 \text{ NSM} = 66.8 \text{ or } 67 \text{ occupants}$$

So, the occupant load of the Student Lounge alone is 67.

Now, you must consider the adjacent spaces. First, look at the Assembly Hall. As you can see on the floor plan, one of the exits from the Assembly Hall empties into the Student Lounge. The number of occupants that will use that exit must pass through the Student Lounge before they reach their final exit, so they must be included in the occupant load of this space. You have been given two separate occupant loads for this space because this space is used in two different ways. Sometimes it is used with tables and chairs (for example for a luncheon) and sometimes it is used with only chairs (for example for a lecture). These different uses would result in different occupant loads. You must use the occupant load that results in the highest concentration of people which is an occupant load of 171. Since there are two exits, you can assume that half of the 171 occupants or 86 occupants would exit into the Student Lounge from the Assembly Hall. So the number of occupants that the Assembly Hall will contribute to the Student Lounge is 86.

Next you must consider the Library. One of the two exits empties into the Student Lounge. You are told that the occupant load of the Library is 36. Again, you can assume that half of the occupants will exit from each exit, so the number of occupants that the Library will contribute to the Student Lounge is 18.

The Administrative Offices have no direct exits to the exterior. In this case, all of the 15 occupants from this area must exit into the Student Lounge to reach an exit. So the number of occupants that the Administrative Offices will contribute to the Student Lounge is 15.

To calculate the final occupant load for the Student Lounge, you now add the occupant loads of each of the areas together: 67 + 86 + 18 + 15 = 186. The occupant load of the Student Lounge area is 186. (*Note:* No occupants are attributed to the toilet facilities because those occupants are already included in the occupant loads for the other areas.)

PROBLEM 5

a. Occupant load of Figure 2.4 = 144.

Explanation: A church is considered an Assembly (A-3) occupancy. Since you are told that this church has permanent continuous pews, you would look on the table under "Assembly with fixed seats." However, instead of giving you a square footage factor, this refers you to another section of the code. (In the 2003 *IBC*, this section is incorrectly identified. It should reference 1004.7 for information on fixed seats.) From what you have learned about determining the occupant load with fixed seats, you know that this section of the code indicates that the occupant load for fixed seats is typically determined by counting the fixed seats. However, since the pews do not have dividing arms, the capacity of the seats is based on one person for every 18 inches (457 mm) of seating length, as explained in the *Guidebook*.

You are told that each pew is 14'-6" (4419.6 mm) long. However, this dimension includes the 3-inch (76.2 mm) thick arms at each end. The actual sitting length is 14 feet, or 168 inches (14 × 12 inches) or 4267 mm. To determine how many persons are allowed on one pew, divide 168 by the 18 inches (4257 by 457 mm) per person. You get 9.3 people. But a fraction of a person cannot sit down, so you must round down to 9 persons per pew. (This is illustrated by the drawing in Figure 2.4a.)

The church floor plan shows that there are 16 equal-size pews. To get the total occupant load for the church, multiply these 16 pews by 9 to get 144.

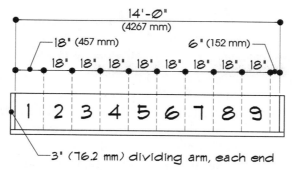

Figure 2.4A. Continuous Pews (Answer)

b. Occupant load of Figure 2.4 with dividing arms = 128.

Explanation: Instead of having continuous pews like the first part of this problem, each pew is now divided into individual seats by dividing arms. Therefore, instead of dividing the length of the pew by 18 inches, you know that the codes tell you to count the actual seats. Figure 2.5 shows that there are 8 seats per pew. Multiply this by the 16 pews shown in the floor plan and you get an occupant load for the space of 128 (8 × 16 = 128).

PROBLEM 6

a. No, because the total area required for this many units is 10,800 square feet (1003.3 s m). This is more than the 9200 square feet (854.7 s m) of the building (*or* because 9200 square feet (854.7 s m) allows only 46 occupants. The developer wants to house 54 occupants).

Explanation: Your first step is to figure the total expected number of occupants (or occupant load). To do this, you multiply the number of units by the number of people per unit:

$$4 \text{ units} \times 1 \text{ person} = 4$$
$$8 \text{ units} \times 4 \text{ people} = 32$$
$$3 \text{ units} \times 6 \text{ people} = \underline{18}$$
$$\text{Total occupants} = 54$$

Next, determine the load factor using the code table. An apartment complex is considered a Residential occupancy; therefore, the load factor is 200 gross square feet (18.58 s m). Then, using the occupant load formula, determine the required floor area:

$$\text{Occupant load} = \text{Floor area} \div \text{Load factor}$$
$$\text{Floor area} = \text{Load factor} \times \text{Occupant load}$$
$$\text{Floor area} = 200 \text{ GSF} \times 54 \text{ occupants} = 10,800 \text{ gross square feet}$$

or

$$\text{Floor area} = 18.58 \text{ GSM} \times 54 \text{ occupants} = 1003.3 \text{ gross square meters}$$

This indicates that the area necessary by the codes for 54 occupants is larger than the area of the building.

Alternate Explanation: Using the same formula and load factor, you can also determine how many occupants are allowed in the 9200 square foot (854.7 s m) building:

$$\text{Occupant load} = \text{Floor area} \div \text{Load factor}$$
$$\text{Occupant load} = 9200 \text{ GSF} \div 200 \text{ GSF} = 46 \text{ occupants}$$

or

$$\text{Occupant load} = 854.7 \text{ GSM} \div 18.58 \text{ GSM} = 46 \text{ occupants}$$

This indicates that the area provided by the existing building will only accommodate 46 occupants.

b. Yes, because the 8400 square feet (780.4 s m) required for a retirement center with this many occupants is within the 9200 square feet (854.7 s m) of the building (*or* because a 9200 square foot (854.7 s m) building allows 75 occupants for a retirement center but the developer wants to house only 70).

Explanation: Use the occupant load formula to find the floor area required for a retirement center with this many occupants. The occupant load is the total expected number of occupants, including tenants and employees: 62 + 8 = 70 occupants. The load factor of 120 gross square feet (11.148 s m) is found in the code table under Institutional occupancy with the subheading of "Sleeping areas." (*Note:* This building is not strictly residential, because health services will be provided. This would need to be considered in the final occupant load calculations. However, in this case, it would not affect the final allowable use.) Plug these figures into the formula to determine how many square feet (or square meters) are required.

$$\text{Occupant load} = \text{Floor area} \div \text{Load factor}$$

$$\text{Floor area} = \text{Load factor} \times \text{Occupant load}$$

$$\text{Floor area} = 120 \text{ GSF} \times 70 \text{ occupants} = 8400 \text{ gross square feet}$$

or

$$\text{Floor area} = 11.148 \text{ GSM} \times 70 \text{ occupants} = 780.4 \text{ gross square meters}$$

This indicates that the floor area necessary for the desired occupant load is within the area of the existing building.

Alternate Explanation: You can also use the same formula and load factor to determine the maximum number of occupants allowed in a 9200 square foot (854.7 s m) building:

$$\text{Occupant load} = \text{Floor area} \div \text{Load factor}$$

$$\text{Occupant load} = 9200 \text{ GSF} \div 120 \text{ GSF} = 76.6 = 77 \text{ occupants}$$

or

$$\text{Occupant load} = 854.7 \text{ GSM} \div 11.148 \text{ GSM} = 76.6, \text{ or } 77 \text{ occupants}$$

This indicates that the area of the building will allow more occupants than necessary.

c. No, because even though the first floor is within the area requirements, the second floor is not (*or* because the expected occupant load for the second floor is higher than that allowed by the codes).

Explanation: A retail center is considered a Mercantile occupancy on the code table. However, Mercantile is further divided into "Basement and grade floor areas," with a load factor of 30 gross square feet (2.79 s m), and "Areas on other floors," with a load factor of 60 gross square feet (5.574 s m). Both apply to the proposed retail center. Use these load factors and the expected number of occupants to determine the required square feet (or area) for each floor:

First Floor:

$$\text{Occupant load} = \text{Floor area} \div \text{Load factor}$$

$$\text{Floor area} = \text{Load factor} \times \text{Occupant load}$$

$$\text{Floor area} = 30 \text{ GSF} \times 125 \text{ occupants} = 3750 \text{ gross square feet}$$

or

$$\text{Floor area} = 2.79 \text{ GSM} \times 125 \text{ occupants} = 348.8 \text{ gross square meters}$$

Second Floor:

$$\text{Occupant load} = \text{Floor area} \div \text{Load factor}$$

$$\text{Floor area} = \text{Load factor} \times \text{Occupant load}$$

$$\text{Floor area} = 60 \text{ GSF} \times 85 \text{ occupants} = 5100 \text{ gross square feet}$$

or

$$\text{Floor area} = 5.574 \text{ GSM} \times 85 \text{ occupants} = 473.8 \text{ gross square meter}$$

Each floor in the building has 4600 square feet (427.3 s m). The first floor calculation falls within this, at 3750 square feet (348.8 s m). The calculation for the second floor requires 5100 square feet (473.8 s m), which is too high.

Alternate Explanation: You can also use the same formula and load factors to determine the maximum number of occupants allowed on each of the 4600 square feet (427.3 s m) floors:

First Floor:

$$\text{Occupant load} = \text{Floor area} \div \text{Load factor}$$

$$\text{Occupant load} = 4600 \text{ GSF} \div 30 \text{ GSF} = 153.3 = 154 \text{ occupants}$$

or

$$\text{Occupant load} = 427.3 \text{ GSM} \div 2.79 \text{ GSM} = 153.2 = 154 \text{ occupants}$$

Second Floor:

$$\text{Occupant load} = \text{Floor area} \div \text{Load factor}$$

$$\text{Occupant load} = 4600 \text{ GSF} \div 60 \text{ GSF} = 76.6 = 77 \text{ occupants}$$

or

$$\text{Occupant load} = 427.3 \text{ GSM} \div 5.574 \text{ GSM} = 76.7 = 77 \text{ occupants}$$

The expected number of 125 occupants falls within the maximum of 154 required by codes on the first floor. However, the 85 occupants on the second floor are above the 77 occupants allowed by the code. So this building will not accommodate the desired occupant load. (*Note:* Strictly speaking, the building could not be used as intended by the owner. However, if a lower occupant load was acceptable on the second floor, then the building could be used as a Mercantile use.)

☐ CHAPTER 3. Construction Types and Building Sizes

PROBLEM 1

a. A designates a "protected" structure and B indicates an "unprotected" structure.

Explanation: Although it is not stated directly in the table, the "A" and "B" in this table indicate when additional fire protection has been added to a structural system. This typically results in an additional 1-hour of fire-resistance rating of the structural components of the building. For example, you can see this by comparing Type IIIA to Type IIIB. (*Note:* Protected and unprotected do not have anything to do with whether the building has an automatic sprinkler system. See the discussion of protected and unprotected in the *Guidebook* in Chapter 3.)

b. 1 Hour.

Explanation: Find the column for Type V and the subcolumn for A (protected). When you cross-reference that to the row titled "Structural frame, including columns, girders, trusses," you will find that a 1-hour fire-resistance rating is required for that building element.

c. 1 hour or the use of an automatic sprinkler system.

Explanation: Find the column for Type II and the subcolumn for A (protected). When you cross-reference that to the row titled, "Bearing walls, Interior" you will find that a 1-hour rating is required. However, if you refer to the note indicated at "A," you are told that an approved automatic sprinkler system can be substituted for the 1-hour fire-resistance-rated construction.

d. Type I, protected (A) or unprotected (B).

Explanation: "Floor construction, Including supporting beams and joists" is listed in the building elements column. Compare the requirements for these elements for each of the construction types. Type I is the only construction type with a rating this high.

e. Interior nonbearing walls or partitions.

Explanation: Locate "Nonbearing walls and partitions, Interior" under the building elements column. If you follow that row under all the construction types, you can see that no construction type requires a non-(load)-bearing partition in the interior of a building to be rated. (*Note:* These partitions may be required to be rated for other reasons within the building codes but not because of the construction type.)

PROBLEM 2

a. No, because this building type (R-1) cannot have more than 16,000 square feet (1486.4 s m) per floor under this type of construction. 17,500 square feet (1626 s m) exceeds the allowable amount.

Explanation: Looking at the left side of the table under "Group," a hotel would fall under the Residential use group "R-1." (See Appendix A.1.) Under this category on the code table, a "Type IIIB" building cannot be more than four stories high with a maximum of 16,000 square feet (1486.4 s m) per floor. The number of stories in this existing building is allowable, the square footage is not.

b. No, because although the number of square feet is noted as "UL" (unlimited) for this use (R-3) and construction type, the code allows only three stories in this type of construction. (There are other factors to be considered as well.)

Explanation: A townhouse or single family home falls under the use group "R-3" on the table. (See Appendix A.1.) When cross-referenced with construction "Type VB," R-3 requires the building to be no more than three stories. In this case, the townhouses that are planned to be built four stories could not be built using Type VB construction. However, if you cross-reference this use with a more fire-resistant construction type, you can see that the townhouses would be allowed to be constructed four stories high if at least Type III construction was used. (Type IV, Heavy Timber would typically not be used in Residential occupancies.) Also notice that the townhouses that were planned to be three stories could be built using Type VB construction; however, they may be regulated by the *International Residential Code (IRC)* instead of the *IBC*. In all cases, the area is noted as unlimited for all construction types for R-3.

c. No, because the total square feet of the first floor of the existing building is more than what the code allows for this type of occupancy (F-2) in the existing construction type. 19,250 square feet (1788 s m) exceeds the maximum of 18,000 square feet (1672 s m) allowed by the code table.

Explanation: If you calculate the number of square feet required for this factory using the occupant load formula, you will determine that your client's factory will require 10,000 square feet (929 s m):

$$\text{Occupant load} = \text{Floor area} \div \text{Load factor}$$

$$\text{Floor area} = \text{Load factor} \times \text{Occupant load}$$

$$\text{Floor area} = 100 \text{ GSF} \times 100 \text{ occupants} = 10,000 \text{ gross square feet}$$

or

$$\text{Floor area} = 9.29 \text{ GSM} \times 100 \text{ occupants} = 929 \text{ gross square meter}$$

Based on this alone, it looks like the space will work. However, on the code table, a low-hazard factory is under "F-2." When you cross reference with "Type IIIB," this category allows no more than three stories with a maximum of 18,000 square feet (1672 s m) per story. The existing building has 19,250 gross square feet (1788 s m) on each floor, which is more than the 18,000 square feet (1672 s m) allowed by the code. (*Note:* Increases in area are allowed by the codes when an automatic sprinkler systems is installed throughout the building, which may make this use possible.)

CHAPTER 4. Means of Egress

PROBLEM 1

Most of these answers can be found in the various diagrams, as shown in Figures 4.5, 4.6, 4.7, and 4.8 of *The Codes Guidebook for Interiors.*

A. Riser height = 7 inches (180 mm) maximum (or 4–7 inches (100–180 mm))

B. Tread length = 11 inches (280 mm) minimum

C. Nosing projection = 1½ inches (38 mm) maximum

D. Stairway rise without landing = 12 feet (3660 mm) maximum

E. Height of handrail = 34–38 inches (865–965 mm)

F. Top handrail extension = 12 inches (305 mm) minimum

G. Bottom handrail extension = tread (B) + 12 inches (305 mm) minimum (or B + F) (*Note:* New editions of ADA guidelines and ICC/ANSI standard may allow the extension to equal the depth of one tread.)

H. Diameter of handrail = 1¼–2 inches (32–51 mm)

I. Minimum ceiling height = 90 inches (2286 mm) minimum

J. Minimum headroom height = 80 inches (2032 mm) minimum

PROBLEM 2

a. Basement = 2 exits
First Floor = 4 exits
Second Floor = 4 exits
Third Floor = 4 exits
Fourth Floor = 4 exits
Fifth Floor = 3 exits
Sixth Floor = 3 exits
Seventh Floor = 3 exits
Eighth Floor = 2 exits

Explanation: When determining the number of exits for an entire floor, remember that the quantity is also affected by the number of occupants on the floor(s) above. In this problem, the fourth floor had the highest occupant load (over 1000 = 4 exits). Since the number of exits cannot decrease as a person travels toward the exit discharge, there must be four exits on the third, second, and first floors as well (even though these floors do not need this many exits).

The fifth floor requires three exits (500–1000 = 3 exits). The sixth floor needs only two exits (1–500 = 2 exits). But since the seventh floor above requires three, the sixth floor requires three exits as well. The eighth floor is not affected by any other floor. The number of exits in the basement is not affected by the floors above, since it is below the main exit discharge at grade level. (Note, however, that when calculating the width of the exits, the occupant load of the basement may affect the exits on the first floor.)

b. 1. 250 feet (76,200 mm); using Table 1015.1.

Explanation: The restaurant on the first floor would be considered an Assembly (A-2) occupancy. (See Appendix A.1.) According to the *IBC* Table 1015.1, in a sprinklered building, the maximum travel distance is 250 feet (76,200 mm).

2. 100 feet (30,480 mm); using Table 1018.2.

Explanation: Office spaces would be considered a Business (B) occupancy. In the *IBC* Table 1018.2, a Business occupancy with one story indicates a maximum of 75 feet (22,860 mm) in the chart (with a minimum occupant load of 50). However, you must refer to footnote "d," which states that if the building has an automatic sprinkler system, the maximum travel distance in a Group B occupancy is 100 feet (30,480 mm).

3. 250 feet (76,200 mm); using Table 1015.1.

Explanation: The wholesale retail shops would be considered a Mercantile (M) occupancy. For sprinklered buildings, the *IBC* Table 1015.1 allows a maximum travel distance of 250 feet (76,200 mm).

4. 75 feet (22,860 mm); using Table 1018.2.

Explanation: The wholesale retail shops would be considered a Mercantile (M) occupancy. For a two-story building, the *IBC* Table 1018.2 allows a maximum travel distance of 75 feet (22,860 mm) as long as the occupant load is 30 or less.

5. 300 feet (91,440 mm); using Table 1015.1.

Explanation: The third through the seventh floors would be considered Business (B) occupancies. For sprinklered buildings, the *IBC* Table 1015.1 allows a maximum travel distance of 300 feet (91,440 mm).

PROBLEM 3

a. 64 inches (1626 mm); 32 inches (815 mm); because even though the formula suggests that the total required width should be 26 inches (660 mm) and thus require only 13½ inches (343 mm) of width at each exit, the *IBC* and accessibility regulations require all exit doors to provide at least a 32-inch (815 mm) clear opening. (This is typically accomplished with a 36-inch (915 mm) wide door.)

Explanation: To determine the required exit width, you multiply the occupant load by the egress variable found on the *IBC* table. For this building, you would refer to the section of the table titled "With Sprinkler System" because you were told that a sprinkler system was added in the renovation of the building. Then, because you are determining the width of the doors (not a stair component), you would use the exit width factor found under the column titled, "Other egress components (inches per occupant)." Since the telemarketing company is a Business (B) occupancy, you can find the variable of 0.15 in the row noted as "Occupancies other than those listed below."

   Multiply this by the occupant load of 175, and you get 26.25, or 26 inches (660 mm). This is the total width required. Since two exits are required from the space, you divide the 26 inches (660 mm) of width between the two exit locations. This equals approximately 13 inches (330 mm) per exit door. However, the codes require a minimum of 32 inches (815 mm) for an exit in most occupancy classifications. (It is also the minimum required by the ADA and ICC/ANSI standard.) In this case, a standard 36-inch (915 mm) door will provide a 32-inch clear opening in each location.

b. 44 inches (1118 mm); because the calculated exit stair width was less than the minimum exit stair width required by the codes, this is the minimum width.

Explanation: The exit stairs serve the entire floor, so to determine the calculated width, you must first determine the total occupant load for the floor. The occupant load for each space has been given on the plan in Figure 4.3: 36 + 50 + 175 + 45 = 306 total occupants. Next, you need to look up the stair variable on the *IBC* table. Looking under the section for "With Sprinkler System," you will find the exit width variable column for "Stairways (inches per occupant)." A Business (B) occupancy would be included in the occupancy group noted as "Occupancies other than those listed below," so the variable of 0.2 for stairway width is used.

   Multiply the total occupant load of 306 by 0.2 to get 61.2, or 61 inches (1549 mm). Since there are two stairways serving this floor, this figure can be divided by two. The calculated minimum width for each stairway is 30½ inches (775 mm) wide. However, from what you know about mean of egress codes, you know that a 44-inch (1118 mm) minimum width is typically required for stairways. In this case, the minimum requirement will determine the required width, not the calculated width. (*Note:* If an area of refuge was adjacent to the stair or located within the stair, a minimum of 48 inches (1220 mm) would be required.)

c. 44 inches (1118 mm); because even though the formula requires a corridor width of 23 inches (584 mm), the *IBC* requires it to be a minimum of 44 inches.

   Explanation: To determine the corridor width for the entire floor, you use the "Other egress components (inches per occupant)" of 0.15 (see Explanation to 'a') and the total occupant load of 306. (See Explanation to 'b' above.) Multiply the total occupant load of 306 by 0.15 to get 46 inches (1168 mm). Since there are two stairways serving this floor, this number can be divided by two. So the calculated minimum width for the corridor is 23 inches (584 mm) wide. However, from what you know about codes, you know that a 44-inch minimum width is required for corridors. In this case, the minimum requirement, not the calculated width, will determine the required width. (*Note:* Accessibility requirements would also require the corridors leading up to the exit stairs to be wider than 23 inches (584 mm) to allow for the necessary clearance at the jamb side of the stairway doors. Wider turnaround areas may also be required.)

PROBLEM 4

Figure 4.4a is the same floor plan of the classroom/seminar room shown to scale at 1/8″ =1′-0″. The various dimensions have been added to the plan for your use in calculating the aisle accessway widths.

a. 31 inches (787 mm); the minimum width of 12 inches (305 mm) for tables between 6 and 12 feet (1829–3658 mm) is added to the 19 inches (483 mm) required by codes for the chair.

   Explanation: First, you must determine the length of Aisle Accessway A. (Remember that the length of the aisle accessway is measured to the middle of the last chair.) Using the 1/8-inch scale, you can measure the length of the aisle accessway. It is approximately 8′-8″ (2642 mm) long. At this length, according to the

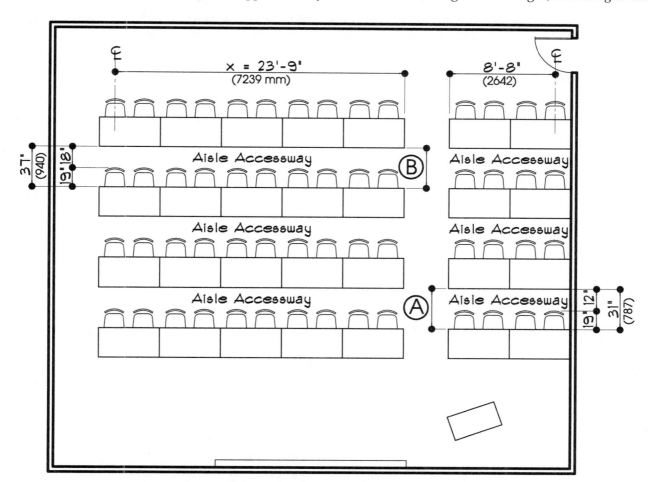

Figure 4.4A. Access Aisleway Widths: Training Room (Answer) (Scale: 1/8″ = 1′-0″)

chart for an aisle accessway between the length of 6 and 12 feet (1829–3658 mm), the required minimum aisle width is 12 inches (305mm). This is the distance between the chair back and the table edge. Because you were asked to give the minimum distance between the tables, this dimension is then added to the 19 inch (483 mm) increment required in the codes to allow for the chair. (See Figure 4.4a.) Since 12 + 19 = 31 inches (305 mm + 483 mm = 788 mm), the total width required between the tables is 31 inches (787 mm).

b. 37 inches (940 mm); the calculated width of 18 inches (457 mm) is added to the 19 inches (483 mm) required by the codes for the chair.

Explanation: First, measure the length of the aisle accessway at Aisle Accessway B using your 1/8-inch scale. (Remember, the length of the aisle accessway is measured to the middle of the last chair.) It is approximately 23'-9" (7239 mm). Since the length of this row is between 12 and 30 feet (3658–9144 mm), the equation given in the chart for calculating the width of the aisle accessway must be used to determine the required aisle accessway width. "x" in the equation is the length of the aisle accessway which you have determined to be 23'-9" (7239 mm).

$$12 \text{ inches} + 0.5\,(x - 12 \text{ feet})$$
$$12 \text{ inches} + 0.5\,(23'\text{-}9'' - 12 \text{ feet})$$
$$12 \text{ inches} + 0.5\,(11'\text{-}9'')$$
$$12 \text{ inches} + 0.5\,(11.75 \text{ feet})$$
$$12 \text{ inches} + 5.875 = 17.875 = 18 \text{ inches} \ (454 \text{ mm})$$

Since you have been asked for the required minimum distance between the tables, you must add this calculated width to the 19 inches (483 mm) required in the codes to allow for the chair. The minimum width required for this aisle accessway is 18 + 19 = 37 inches (940 mm). (*Note:* In the equation the 0.5 inches must be multiplied by the number of feet or a fraction thereof; 9 inches equals 0.75 feet (9 ÷ 12).)

PROBLEM 5

Figure 4.5a is the same floor plan of the doctor's office shown to scale at 1/8" = 1'-0". The floor plan has been faded to the background so you can clearly see the answers. Each of the drawn lines has a different designation and is marked with the corresponding letter of the answer.

a. 34'-0" (10,363.2 mm), because the minimum required distance is half of the longest diagonal in the space.

Explanation: Using the "half diagonal rule," first you find the longest diagonal in the space using a straight line. This is shown by line A in the floor plan. If you use your 1/8-inch scale, the length of this line is 68'-0" (20,726.4 mm). Half of this line will give you the minimum distance required between the two exits. (*Note:* If the building had an automatic sprinkler system the required separation distance may be reduced to one third of the overall diagonal of the space.)

b. 67'-6" (20,574 mm) This is accurate within 1 foot (305 mm).

Explanation: Travel distance is defined as the maximum distance a person should have to travel from any position in a building or space to the nearest exit. To clearly show which travel distance is the longest, two have been measured on the floor plan in Figure 4.5a, each from the furthest corners from the exit. B1 starts in Exam 5 and B2 starts in Exam 2.

To measure the travel distance, start 1 foot from the furthest corner of the room and draw straight lines along the center line of the natural path of travel (i.e., center line of the corridor). Take the most direct route to the exit, keeping at least 1 foot away from all walls and door jambs. Draw the lines to the center line of each doorway, ending with the center of the exit door. After you draw all your lines, measure each straight line separately and put the dimensions directly on the floor plan. If you add up the dimensions for each line section, you get a travel distance for B1 of 67'-6" (20,574 mm) and B2 of 63'-0" (19,202.4 mm). Since B1 is the longest, it is the answer. (*Note:* All lines in this example are in 6-inch (152 mm) increments for ease of calculation.)

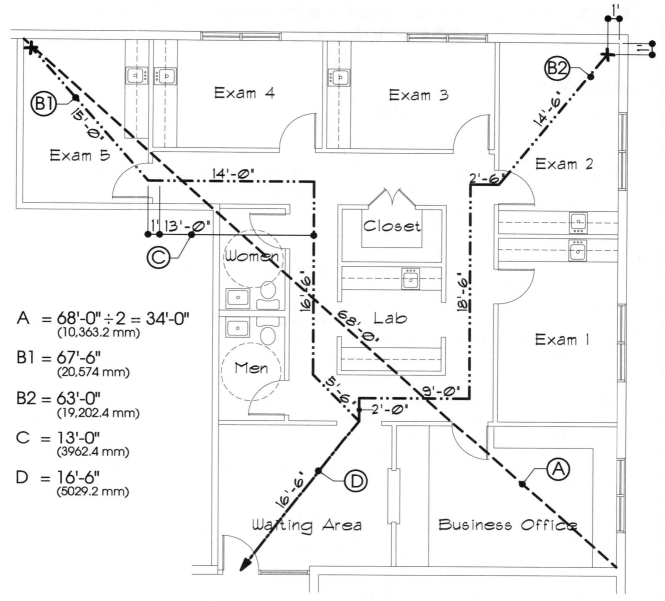

A $= 68'-0'' \div 2 = 34'-0''$
(10,363.2 mm)

B1 $= 67'-6''$
(20,574 mm)

B2 $= 63'-0''$
(19,202.4 mm)

C $= 13'-0''$
(3962.4 mm)

D $= 16'-6''$
(5029.2 mm)

Figure 4.5A. Travel Distances: Doctor's Office (Answer)
(Scale: 1/8" = 1'-0"; 1 square foot = 0.0929 square meter)

c. Yes, 13'-0" (3962.4 mm); Yes, because a dead-end corridor is typically allowed by the codes in a nonsprinklered building if it is under 20'-0" (6096 mm).

   Explanation: A dead-end corridor is a corridor with only one direction of exit, like the corridor leading to Exam 5. To measure the dead-end corridor, you start 1 foot from the end of the corridor, which, in this case, is at the door to Exam 5. Then follow the natural path of travel to the center line of the corridor that provides two directions to the exit. See the dimension line marked C on the floor plan. (*Note:* If the building was sprinklered, a longer dead-end corridor length may be allowed.)

d. Yes, Waiting Area, 16'-6" (5029.2 mm).

   Explanation: A common path of travel is defined as an exit access where two paths merge to become one. This occurs in the Waiting Area as shown by the letter D on the floorplan. It is where the two corridors merge on the way to the exit door.

CHAPTER 5. Fire-Resistant Materials and Assemblies

PROBLEM 1

Hourly fire resistance rating of wall assemblies:

A. 2 hours; using Table 302.3.2.

   Explanation: This is an occupancy separation wall because it separates the Business (B) and Mercantile (M) occupancies. To determine the required rating, you must refer to the *IBC* Table 302.3.2. Look under the "Use" column to locate the row "B" for Business. Then cross-reference this row with the "M" column for Mercantile along the top of the table. Where the row and column meet indicates that a 2-hour rating is required.

B. No rating; using Table 1016.1.

   Explanation: Typically, fire-resistance rated walls are not required in small tenant spaces. However, to confirm this with the information in the code, refer to the *IBC* Table 1016.1. The wall indicated on the plan is a corridor wall within the tenant space in a Business (B) use. Find "B" under the column for "Occupancy." You can see that the table only gives information for exit access corridors that serve an occupant load of more than 30. Because you are told that the occupant load is only 13, in this case, the corridor walls would not be required to be rated.

C. 1 hour; using Table 1016.1.

   Explanation: This is a corridor wall and is considered an exit access corridor. Refer to the *IBC* Table 1016.1. Business (B) and Mercantile (M) occupancies are included in the same group under the "Occupancy" column. Because you can determine that the exit access corridor serves an occupant load of 91 (13 + 14 + 12 + 7 + 45) and you were told that the building is unsprinklered, the corridor is required to have a fire-resistance rating of 1 hour. (*Note:* If the building had been sprinklered, the exit access corridor would not have been required to be rated.)

D. 1 hour; using Table 1016.

   Explanation: This is a corridor wall and is considered an exit access corridor. The same information as noted in item C above applies. (*Note:* Some jurisdictions may allow restroom walls to be nonrated.)

E. 2 hour; (no code table).

   Explanation: This wall is part of the fire barriers that enclose the elevator. An elevator wall is considered a type of shaft enclosure. From what you know about the codes, the codes require elevator shafts to be rated 2 hours when they extend more than three floors. The portion of this enclosure that is part of the exit access corridor must also be rated 2 hours.

F. 1 hour (or an automatic sprinkler system); using Table 302.1.1.

   Explanation: On the floor plan, you are told that the area of the storage room is 150 square feet (14 s m). Refer to the *IBC* Table 302.1.1. In the column titled "Room or Area" you find "Storage rooms over 100 square feet." Since the room is over 100 square feet (9.3 s m), it is considered an incidental use. To determine the required rating, look at under the column titled "Separation." You see that for this use a 1-hour rated wall is required. The table also tells you that an automatic fire-extinguishing system within the room may be substituted for the rated walls.

G. 1 hour (or an automatic sprinkler system); using Table 302.1.1.

   Explanation: Refer to the *IBC* Table 302.1. 1. In the column titled "Room or Area" you can find "Waste and linen collection rooms over 100 square feet." Since the area of this trash room is 120 square feet (11.1 s m), it is considered an incidental use. If you look at the column titled "Separation," you see that for this use a

1-hour rated wall is required. The table also tells you that an automatic fire-extinguishing system within the room may be substituted for the rated walls.

H. 2 hour; (no code table).

Explanation: This wall is part of the exit access corridor; however, it is also part of the exit stairway. This wall is part of the fire barriers that enclose the exit stair. From what you know about the codes, the codes require stairways to be rated 2 hours when they extend more than three floors. The portion of this enclosure that is part of the exit access corridor must also be rated 2 hours.

Hourly fire rating of opening protectives:

1. ⅓ hour or 20-minute; using Table 715.3.

Explanation: This door is in the exit access corridor wall. You have already determined that the exit access corridor for this building requires a 1-hour rating. Now refer to the *IBC* Table 715.3. Under the column for "Type of Assembly" find "Fire partitions: Corridor walls." Then, locate a 1-hour rating under the column for "Required Assembly Rating (hours)." Follow that over to the column titled "Minimum Fire Door and Fire Shutter Assembly Rating (hours)" and you will find that a ⅓ hour rating is required. This is commonly referred to a 20-minute door.

2. No rating; (no code table).

Explanation: Since the walls in the tenant space do not require a fire rating, neither do the doors located in these walls.

3. ¾ hour; using Table 715.3.

Explanation: This door is located in wall that is the exit access corridor which you have determined must be rated 1 hour. And, it is part of the enclosure to the incidental use "Storage rooms over 100 square feet," which you have determined must be rated 1 hour as well. (For this example, we will assume the option of providing an automatic extinguishing system is not being used.) Refer to the *IBC* Table 715.3 to determine the rating of the door. Under the "Type of Assembly," you find two options for interior walls rated 1 hour: "Fire barriers having a required fire-resistance rating of 1 hour" and "Fire partitions." From what you know about the codes, you know the exit access corridor walls would be considered fire partitions. However, the walls enclosing the incidental use room would be considered fire barriers. Fire barriers have more stringent requirements than fire partitions. Since this wall does both, you must use the requirements for fire barriers. There are two types of fire barriers listed in the table. Because these walls do not enclose a shaft, the "Other fire barriers" is the correct type of fire barrier. You can then determine that a ¾ hour door is required.

4. 1½ hour; using Table 715.3.

Explanation: This door is within the stairway enclosure. You have already determined that the walls surrounding the stairway require a 2-hour rating. Now refer to the *IBC* Table 715.3. Under the column titled "Type of Assembly," the first row is "Fire walls and fire barriers having a required fire-resistance rating greater than 1 hour." Find the 2-hour rating under "Required Assembly Rating (hours)" and you can determine that a 1½ hour rated door is required.

5. ⅓ hour or 20 minutes; using Table 715.3.

Explanation: This door is located within the exit access corridor that you have already determined to be rated 1 hour. The same information as noted in item 1 above applies. (*Note:* Some jurisdictions may allow restroom doors to be nonrated.)

6. 1½ hour; using Table 715.3.

Explanation: This door is located in the shaft enclosure that is more than three stories. You have already determined that the walls surrounding this elevator require a 2-hour rating. The same information as noted in item 4 above applies.

7. ¾ hour; using Table 715.3.

   Explanation: Similar to item 3 above, this door is located in wall that is the exit access corridor that you have determined must be rated 1 hour. And, it is also part of the enclosure to an incidental use room "Waste and linen collection rooms over 100 square feet." The same information as noted in item 3 above applies.

8. 1½ hours; using Table 715.3.

   Explanation: It is indicated by the plan that this opening is within the actual refuse chute. This type of opening would be considered part of a shaft enclosure. Because we must assume that it extends through all the building floors, the shaft enclosure would require a rating of 2 hours like the elevators and the stairway enclosures. The same information as noted in item 4 above applies to this answer.

PROBLEM 2

a. 1 hour; No, an automatic fire extinguishing system is not required.

   Explanation: "Waste and linen collection rooms over 100 square feet" is a category shown toward the bottom of the *IBC* Table 302.1.1. Since you were told that the area of the room is 250 square feet (23 s m) these requirements would apply. This category requires a 1-hour fire rating. It does not require an automatic fire extinguishing system if the fire resistance rated partitions are provided. However, you could provide an automatic sprinkler system within the area instead of the rated partitions. (Note "a" at the bottom of the table tells you that the automatic fire-extinguishing system is only required to be installed in the room, not in the entire building.)

b. No.

   Explanation: "Storage rooms over 100 square feet" are called out in this table. However, either a 1-hour rated partition can be used or an automatic fire-extinguishing system can be used. The codes require one or the other but not both.

c. No, it is not allowed in I-2 occupancies.

   Explanation: A hospital is an I-2 occupancy classification. (See Figure A.1 in Appendix.) The "Room or Area" designation for "Group I-2 waste and linen collection rooms" indicates that a 1-hour separation is required. It does not give you the option of an automatic fire-extinguishing system instead of the rated partitions. (*Note:* This is because in most cases, hospitals are required to be sprinklered by the codes and so this would not provide any additional protection to this room.)

d. Yes; No.

   Explanation: A prison is an I-3 occupancy classification. (See Figure A.1 in Appendix.) The room designation for "Group I-3 cells equipped with padded surfaces" indicates that a 1-hour separation is required. It does not give you the option of an automatic fire-extinguishing system instead of the rated partitions. (*Note:* This is because in most cases, prisons, like hospitals, are required to be sprinklered by the codes and so this would not provide any additional protection to this room.)

e. No, because the room is smaller than required to be separated by the code.

   Explanation: According to this table, store rooms are only required to be separated from other areas when the room exceeds 100 square feet (9.3 s m). Since you were told that this storage room is 65 square feet (6 s m), it does not require fire-resistance-rated partitions or an automatic fire-extinguishing system.

PROBLEM 3

a. 1.5 hour.

   Explanation: First, refer to the *IBC* Table 302.1.1 to determine the rating of the walls around the laundry room. Under the "Room or Area" column is the room designation "Laundry rooms over 100 square feet." Refer to the "Separation" column. It tells you that 1-hour partitions are required (or an automatic fire-extinguishing system). For this example, we will assume that the 1-hour partition is provided around the laundry room. Now, refer to Table 716.3.1. Under the column "Type of penetration," find the section called "Less than 3-hour fire-resistance-rated assemblies." The adjacent column indicates that a 1.5-hour minimum damper rating is required in this 1-hour wall.

b. 1 hour.

Explanation: First, refer to the *IBC* Table 302.1.1 to determine the rating of the walls enclosing the incinerator room. In the first column, under "Room or Area" is the use "Incinerator rooms." The partitions around the incinerator room are required to be rated 2 hours (and have an automatic fire-extinguishing system). Now, refer to Table 716.3.1. Under the column "Type of penetration," find the section called "Less than 3-hour fire-resistance-rated assemblies." The adjacent column indicates that a 1.5-hour minimum damper rating is required in this 2-hour wall.

☐ CHAPTER 6. Fire Protection Systems

PROBLEM 1

Below are 21 different automatic sprinkler "trade-offs" that affect interior spaces. Any of these are a possible answer. Many of these trade-offs were listed in the "Common Sprinkler Trade-offs" list in Figure 6.6 of *The Codes Guidebook for Interiors.* Others were mentioned within the text.

1. Lower fire assembly ratings in walls and floor/ceilings assemblies

2. Longer travel distances

3. Larger areas of glazing

4. Reduced number of fire alarms

5. Lower finish class requirements

6. Lower furniture ratings

7. Eliminate firestops behind raised finishes

8. Use of additional foam plastic insulation or trim

9. Longer dead end corridors

10. Open exit access stairways between two and three stories

11. Nonenclosed escalators

12. Omit or reduce rating of fire dampers

13. Reduce draftstops

14. Eliminate or reduce standpipes

15. Allow less fire resistant construction types

16. Reduce the number of fire extinguishers

17. Additional decorative trim

18. Less compartmentation in a high-rise building

19. Lower rating of opening protectives

20. Area of refuge may not be required at accessible elevators and exit stairways

21. Increase in allowable areas

PROBLEM 2

A. Upright

B. Recessed sidewall

C. Pendant

D. Recessed pendant

E. Concealed

F. Sidewall

☐ CHAPTER 7. Plumbing and Mechanical Requirements

PROBLEM 1

Most of these answers can be found in the various diagrams shown in Figure 7.2, Figure 7.3, Figure 7.5, and Figure 7.9 of *The Codes Guidebook for Interiors*. Others are mentioned within the text. (*Note:* Although there may be some minor differences between the codes, the ADA guidelines, and the ICC/ANSI accessibility standard, you were asked to provide the most restrictive requirements in each case.)

A. Depth of lavatory = 17 inches (430 mm) minimum

B. Height of clear knee space = 27 inches (685 mm) minimum

C. Height to bottom of mirror = 40 inches (1015 mm) maximum

D. Height to top of lavatory = 34 inches (865 mm) maximum

E. Length of rear grab bar = 36 inches (915 mm) minimum

F. Distance from side wall to rear grab bar = 6 inches (150 mm) maximum

G. Height to grab bar = 33–36 inches (840–915 mm)

H. Height to top of toilet seat = 17–19 inches (430–485 mm)

I. Distance from center line of toilet to side wall = 18 inches (455 mm) no minimum or maximum

J. Distance from rear wall to side grab bar = 12 inches (305 mm) maximum

K. Diameter of grab bar = 1½ inch maximum (38 mm) or 1¼ to 1½ inches (32–38 mm)

L. Height to center line of toilet paper dispenser = 19 inches (485 mm) minimum

M. Distance from far side of toilet paper dispenser to rear wall = 36 inches (915 mm) maximum

N. Length of side grab bar = 42 inches (1065 mm) minimum

PROBLEM 2

a. 10; there are 3 water closets required for the visitors and 7 water closets required for employees.

   Explanation: A nursing home is shown on the Table 403.1 as an Institutional (I-2) occupancy. First, find "Institutional" under the column titled "Classification." Then locate "I-2." Adjacent to I-2 you can see that there is a separate category for "Employees, other than residential care" and "Visitors, other than residential care" in the "Description" column.

   First, let's look at the requirement for employees. In this row, you see that one water closet is required for 1 per 25 occupants. You are given the occupancy load of 155. 155 divided by 25 = 6.2. Note "a" at the bottom of the table indicates that you must round up for any fraction of a number of persons. So, 7 water closets would be required for the employees. (Also see Note "b," which states that employees must be provided with separate facilities from patients.)

Now, determine the requirements for visitors. The row titled "Visitors, other than residential care" calls for 1 per 75 occupants. The occupant load of 155 is then divided by 75 = 2.06. This number must also be rounded up. So, 3 water closets are required for visitors. A total of 10 water closets (3 + 7) are required for employees and visitors.

b. 1. 16 water closets (8 water closets for male and 8 water closets for female)
   2. 8 lavatories (4 lavatories for male and 4 lavatories for female)
   3. 2 drinking fountains

   Explanation: Find "Assembly" under the "Classification" column in the *IBC* Table 403.1. Nightclubs are listed as "A-2" in the "Use Group" column. For water closets, there are different ratios provided for each gender. (In this case, the ratio is equally distributed between genders with one water closet required for every 40 occupants.) For the occupant load of 600, it is assumed there would be 300 males and 300 females. 300 divided by 40 = 7.5. As instructed in Note "a," you must round the number up to 8. So, eight water closets must be provided for each gender.

   For lavatories the required ratio is 1 per 75. 600 divided by 75 = 8 total. (This would be distributed equally so that 4 lavatories would be for males and 4 lavatories for female.) For drinking fountains the ratio is 1 per 500. 600 divided by 500 = 1.2. Since you need to round up, 2 drinking fountains must be provided. (To meet accessibility requirement, one could be mounted at standing height and one at wheelchair height.)

c. None; no clothes washers are listed as required in the table.

   Explanation: A dormitory would be considered a Residential (R-2). Find "Residential" and "R-2" under the "Classification" and "Use Group" columns. Then find "Dormitories, fraternities, sororities and boarding houses (not transient)" under the "Description" column. Under the column labeled "Other," only one service sink is required. An automatic clothes washer connection is not listed.

d. Two.

   Explanation: An apartment building would be considered Residential (R-2). Find "Residential" and "R-2" in the "Classification" and "Use Group" columns. Under "Other," the requirements indicate 1 automatic clothes washer connection per 20 dwelling units. 40 dwelling units divided by 20 = 2; therefore, two are required.

e. 1 water closet, 1 lavatory, 1 bath tub or shower, 1 kitchen sink, 1 automatic clothes washer connection.

   Explanation: The requirements for a single-family dwelling are found under Residential (R-3), "One- and two-family dwellings." Each required fixture is listed across the table in that row.

f. Females; females have a lower ratio and therefore require more water closets.

   Explanation: An opera house would be an A-1 Assembly. The requirement for water closets for "Assembly" and "A-1" on the table is 1 per 125 for male and 1 per 65 for female. 65 will divide into the occupant load more often than the 125 for males. The requirement for females is greater. (Sometimes these numbers can be amended by local laws. See discussion of potty parity in the *Guidebook* in Chapter 7.)

☐ CHAPTER 8. Electrical and Communication Requirements

There are no Study Problems for this chapter.

☐ CHAPTER 9. Finish and Furniture Selection

PROBLEM 1

This hotel consists of a total of three different occupancy classifications—Residential, Business (or office), and Assembly. Since this is an existing building, each will be classified as an existing occupancy. If you refer to the "Occupancy" column on the left side of the *LSC* table, the hotel itself (i.e., room and suites) would be under "Hotels and Dormitories—Existing." The offices on the floor plan would be listed under "Business and Ambulatory Care—Existing." The third occupancy is for the ballroom, which would be considered an Assembly occupancy. Since you were told in the diagram that the occupancy load of the ballroom is 305, it would be classified as "Assembly—Existing, > 300 occupant load."

1. Main Lobby: Class A only and Class I or II.

   Explanation: Since the Main Lobby acts as an exit for all three occupancies, you need to look under "Exits" for each occupancy and determine which has the strictest requirements. The "Assembly" occupancy is the strictest for the wall and ceiling finishes with a Class A, therefore it is the only one allowed. However, it does not require rated floor finishes. Only the "Hotels and Dormitories" occupancy requires rated floor finishes. They can be either Class I or Class II.

2. Ballroom: Class A or B (no floor rating).

   Explanation: The Ballroom is considered an Assembly occupancy. The Ballroom is not an exit or an exit access, therefore, under "Other Spaces" for "Assembly," Class A or B is allowed. No floor rating is required.

3. Offices: Class A, B, or C (no floor rating).

   Explanation: Under "Other Spaces" for "Business and Ambulatory Health Care," Class A, B, or C is allowed. No floor rating is required.

4. Corridor: Class A or B and Class I or II.

   Explanation: Although it could be argued that this exit access corridor primarily serves the hotel rooms, any of the occupancies could use this corridor to exit. Therefore, you need to look under "Exit Access Corridors" for all three occupancies and determine which has the strictest requirements. All three require Class A or B wall and ceiling finishes. Only the "Hotels and Dormitories" occupancy requires a rated floor finish of either Class I or II.

5. Single Room: Class A, B, or C (no floor rating).

   Explanation: Under "Other Spaces" for "Hotels and Dormitories," Class A, B, or C is allowed. No floor rating is required.

6. Suite: Class A, B, or C (no floor rating).

   Explanation: Similar to the Single Room, the Suite is found under "Other Spaces" for "Hotels and Dormitories." Class A, B, or C is allowed, but no floor rating is required.

7. Vestibule: Class A only and Class I or II.

   Explanation: This is considered an exit or exit passageway. Like the corridor in item 4, any of the three occupancies could use this exit. Therefore, you need to look under "Exits" for each occupancy and determine which has the strictest requirements. The "Assembly" occupancy allows only Class A wall and ceiling finishes. The "Hotels and Dormitories" occupancy requires Class I or II floor finishes.

8. Exit Stair: Class A or B and Class I or II.

   Explanation: This is also considered an exit; however it is an exit for the floors above. Since you were told that all the other floors are strictly hotel rooms, your answer is determined by the "Hotels and Dormitories" occupancy. For "Exits," it requires Class A or B wall and ceiling finishes and Class I or II floor finishes.

PROBLEM 2

a. Class C.

Explanation: Note 6 at the bottom of the table explains what is allowed when a building has an automatic sprinkler system. Basically, the code allows you to reduce the required finish class by one class rating, so that a Class A can become a Class B finish and a Class B can become a Class C finish. In Problem 1, you determined that the least strict wall finish required in the unsprinklered Ballroom is a Class B. Therefore, with sprinklers you can use a finish which is one class rating lower than shown in the table and use a Class C.

b. Class A and Class I or II.

Explanation: This is found under "Exits" in the occupancy category of "Hotels and Dormitories—New."

c. Class A or B.

Explanation: A Gift Shop would be considered a Mercantile occupancy. The answer is found under "Other Spaces" in the "Mercantile—New" occupancy.

d. Class B.

Explanation: This is found under "Other Spaces" in the occupancy category of "Healthcare—Existing." It gives you a choice of Class A or Class B. Class B is the lowest rating.

e. Class I or II.

Explanation: This is found under "Exits" in the occupancy category of "Detention and Correctional—Existing."

f. Class II.

Explanation: Although you are typically allowed to use a lower rated finish when a automatic sprinkler system is used as described in answer 'a' above, sprinklers are mandatory in new "Detention and Correctional" occupancies as noted in the "Occupancy" column. Note 6 also tells you that allowing a lower finish to be used when the building is sprinklered does not apply to detention and correctional occupancies. So, Class II is the lowest level of floor finish allowed.

PROBLEM 3

a. *Pill Test* (or *DOC FF1-70*) (or *ASTM 2859*).

Explanation: Any of these three answers would be correct. They are all the same test. (It is also known as the *Methenamine Pill Test*.) All carpets sold in the United States must pass this test. The *Flooring Radiant Panel Test* would *not* be the correct answer, because it is rarely required in a room or space that is not part of an exit or exit access.

b. *Room Corner Test,* because it is the standard test required for napped, tufted, or looped fabrics and carpets used on walls and ceilings.

c. *NFPA 701* (or *ASTM D6413*) (or *UL 214*), because it is the standard test required for vertical treatments that hang straight, and this tapestry covers more than 10 percent of the wall area.

d. *NFPA 701* (or *ASTM D6413*) (or *UL 214*), because it is the standard test required for vertical treatments that are folded or gathered.

e. *CAL 133,* because in jurisdictions that require furniture to pass *CAL 133,* it is usually required in public spaces with 10 or more seats.

Explanation: For both safety and liability reasons, you should always use the strictest finish and furniture requirements available, even if they are not currently required in your jurisdiction.

f. No test, because the "10 percent rule" typically allows small wall hangings to be nonrated.

Explanation: If you wanted a rated wall hanging, it would need to pass *NFPA 701* (see 'c' above).

g. There are two main choices; any two of the following combinations would be an appropriate answer.
   1. *Steiner Tunnel Test* (or *ASTM E84*) (or *NFPA 255*) (or *UL 723*)
   2. *Smolder Resistance Test* (or *NFPA 260*) (or *CAL 116*) (or *ASTM E1353*)

   Explanation: Other more stringent tests are available that test the entire piece of furniture or furniture assembly (i.e., mockup) but you were only asked for upholstery related tests.

h. *Room Corner Test,* because it is the standard test required for napped, tufted, or looped fabrics and carpets used on walls and ceiling.

i. *ASTM E1590* (or *CAL 129*), because although all mattresses must pass government testing, additional tests are required in certain public occupancies.

☐ CHAPTER 10. Code Officials and the Code Process

There are no Study Problems for this chapter.

APPENDIX A

CODE TABLES

The code tables found in this appendix are also included in *The Codes Guidebook for Interiors*. The corresponding figure number in the *Guidebook* is indicated under each table in this appendix.

Occupancy Classification	ICC International Building Code		NFPA Life Safety Code and **NFPA 5000**	
ASSEMBLY	A-1	Assembly, Theaters (Fixed Seats)	A-A	Assembly, O.L. > 1000
	A-2	Assembly, Food and/or Drink Consumption	A-B	Assembly, O.L. > 300 1000
	A-3	Assembly, Worship, Recreation, Amusement	A-C	Assembly, O.L. ≥ 50 ≤ 300
	A-4	Assembly, Indoor Sporting Events		
	A-5	Assembly, Outdoor Activities		
BUSINESS	B	Business	B	Business
EDUCATION	E	Educational (includes some Day Care)	E	Educational
FACTORY/INDUSTRIAL	F-1	Factory Industrial, Moderate Hazard	I-A	Industrial, General
	F-2	Factory Industrial, Low Hazard	I-B	Industrial, Special Purpose
			I-C	Industrial, High Hazard
HAZARDOUS	H-1	Hazardous, Detonation Hazard		(included in Group I)
	H-2	Hazardous, Deflagration Hazard or Accelerated Burning		
	H-3	Hazardous, Physical or Combustible Hazard		
	H-4	Hazardous, Health Hazard		
	H-5	Hazardous, Hazardous Production Materials (HPM)		
INSTITUTIONAL	I-1	Institutional, Supervised Personal Care, O.L. > 16	D-I	Detentional/Correctional, Free Egress
			D-II	Detentional/Correctional, Zoned Egress
	I-2	Institutional, Health Care	D-III	Detentional/Correctional, Zoned Impeded Egress
	I-3	Institutional, Restrained		
	I-4	Institutional, Day Care Facilities	D-IV	Detentional/Correctional, Impeded Egress
			D-V	Detentional/Correctional, Contained
			H	Health Care
			DC	Day Care
MERCANTILE	M	Mercantile	M-A	Mercantile, > 3 levels or >30,000 sq.ft.
			M-B	Mercantile, floor above or below grade level, or > 3,000 ≤ 30,000 sq.ft.
			M-C	Mercantile, 1 story and ≤ 3,000
RESIDENTIAL	R-1	Residential, Transient	R-A	Residential, Hotels and Dormitories
	R-2	Residential, Multi-Dwelling Unit	R-B	Residential, Apartments
	R-3	Residential, One- and Two-Dwellings Units	R-C	Residential, Lodging or Rooming Houses
	R-4	Residential, Care and Assisted Living Facilities O.L. > 5 ≤ 16	R-D	Residential, One- and Two-Family Dwellings
			R-E	Residential, Board and Care
STORAGE	S-1	Storage, Moderate Hazard	S	Storage
	S-2	Storage, Low Hazard		
UTILITY/MISCELLANEOUS	U	Utility and Miscellaneous		Special Structures and High-rise Buildings

NOTE: The *Life Safety Code* designates between new and existing, the *NFPA 5000* does not.

O.L. = Occupancy Load

APPENDIX A.1. Figure 2.2. Comparison of Occupancy Classifications (This chart is a summary of information contained in the *International Building Code (IBC)*, the *NFPA 5000*, and the *Life Safety Code (LSC)*. Neither the ICC nor the NFPA assume responsibility for the accuracy or the completion of this chart.)

TABLE 1004.1.2
MAXIMUM FLOOR AREA ALLOWANCES PER OCCUPANT

OCCUPANCY	FLOOR AREA IN SQ. FT. PER OCCUPANT
Agricultural building	300 gross
Aircraft hangars	500 gross
Airport terminal 　Baggage claim 　Baggage handling 　Concourse 　Waiting areas	 20 gross 300 gross 100 gross 15 gross
Assembly 　Gaming floors (keno, slots, etc.)	 11 gross
Assembly with fixed seats	See Section 1003.2.2.9
Assembly without fixed seats 　Concentrated (chairs only—not fixed) 　Standing space 　Unconcentrated (tables and chairs)	 7 net 5 net 15 net
Bowling centers, allow 5 persons for each lane including 15 feet of runway, and for additional areas	 7 net
Business areas	100 gross
Courtrooms—other than fixed seating areas	40 net
Dormitories	50 gross
Educational 　Classroom area 　Shops and other vocational room areas	 20 net 50 net
Exercise rooms	50 gross
H-5 Fabrication and manufacturing areas	200 gross
Industrial areas	100 gross
Institutional areas 　Inpatient treatment areas 　Outpatient areas 　Sleeping areas	 240 gross 100 gross 120 gross
Kitchens, commercial	200 gross
Library 　Reading rooms 　Stack area	 50 net 100 gross
Locker rooms	50 gross
Mercantile 　Areas on other floors 　Basement and grade floor areas 　Storage, stock, shipping areas	 60 gross 30 gross 300 gross
Parking garages	200 gross
Residential	200 gross
Skating rinks, swimming pools 　Rink and pool 　Decks	 50 gross 15 gross
Stages and platforms	15 net
Accessory storage areas, mechanical equipment room	 300 gross
Warehouses	500 gross

For SI:　1 square foot = 0.0929 m^2.

APPENDIX A.2. Figure 2.8. *International Building Code® (IBC®)* Table 1004.1.2, Maximum Floor Area Allowances per Occupant (*International Building Code* 2003. Copyright 2002. Falls Church, Virginia: International Code Council, Inc. Reproduced with permission. All rights reserved.)

TABLE 601
FIRE-RESISTANCE RATING REQUIREMENTS FOR BUILDING ELEMENTS (hours)

BUILDING ELEMENT	TYPE I		TYPE II		TYPE III		TYPE IV	TYPE V	
	A	B	A^d	B	A^d	B	HT	A^d	B
Structural frame[a] Including columns, girders, trusses	3^b	2^b	1	0	1	0	HT	1	0

Bearing walls
  Exterior[f]
  Interior
	3
	3^b
		2
		2^b
			1
			1
				0
				0
					2
					1
						2
						0
							2
							1/HT
								1
								1
									0
									0

Nonbearing walls and partitions Exterior	See Table 602								
Nonbearing walls and partitions Interior[e]	0	0	0	0	0	0	See Section 602.4.6	0	0
Floor construction Including supporting beams and joists	2	2	1	0	1	0	HT	1	0
Roof construction Including supporting beams and joists	$1^1/_2{}^c$	1^c	1^c	0	1^c	0	HT	1^c	0

For SI: 1 foot = 304.8 mm.

a. The structural frame shall be considered to be the columns and the girders, beams, trusses and spandrels having direct connections to the columns and bracing members designed to carry gravity loads. The members of floor or roof panels which have no connection to the columns shall be considered secondary members and not a part of the structural frame.

b. Roof supports: Fire-resistance ratings of structural frame and bearing walls are permitted to be reduced by 1 hour where supporting a roof only.

c. 1. Except in Factory-Industrial (F-1), Hazardous (H), Mercantile (M) and Moderate-Hazard Storage (S-1) occupancies, fire protection of structural members shall not be required, including protection of roof framing and decking where every part of the roof construction is 20 feet or more above any floor immediately below. Fire-retardant-treated wood members shall be allowed to be used for such unprotected members.

   2. In all occupancies, heavy timber shall be allowed where a 1-hour or less fire-resistance rating is required.

   3. In Type I and II construction, fire-retardant-treated wood shall be allowed in buildings including girders and trusses as part of the roof construction when the building is:
      i. Two stories or less in height;
      ii. Type II construction over two stories; or
      iii. Type I construction over two stories and the vertical distance from the upper floor to the roof is 20 feet or more.

d. An approved automatic sprinkler system in accordance with Section 903.3.1.1 shall be allowed to be substituted for 1-hour fire-resistance-rated construction, provided such system is not otherwise required by other provisions of the code or used for an allowable area increase in accordance with Section 506.3 or an allowable height increase in accordance with Section 504.2. The 1-hour substitution for the fire resistance of exterior walls shall not be permitted.

e. Not less than the fire-resistance rating required by other sections of this code.

f. Not less than the fire-resistance rating based on fire separation distance (see Table 602).

APPENDIX A.3. Figure 3.1. *International Building Code (IBC)* Table 601, Fire-Resistance Rating Requirements for Building Elements (*International Building Code* 2003. Copyright 2002. Falls Church, Virginia: International Code Council, Inc. Reproduced with permission. All rights reserved.)

TABLE 503
ALLOWABLE HEIGHT AND BUILDING AREAS
Height limitations shown as stories and feet above grade plane.
Area limitations as determined by the definition of "Area, building," per floor.

GROUP	Hgt(feet) Hgt(S)	TYPE I A	TYPE I B	TYPE II A	TYPE II B	TYPE III A	TYPE III B	TYPE IV HT	TYPE V A	TYPE V B
		UL	160	65	55	65	55	65	50	40
A-1	S	UL	5	3	2	3	2	3	2	1
	A	UL	UL	15,500	8,500	14,000	8,500	15,000	11,500	5,500
A-2	S	UL	11	3	2	3	2	3	2	1
	A	UL	UL	15,500	9,500	14,000	9,500	15,000	11,500	6,000
A-3	S	UL	11	3	2	3	2	3	2	1
	A	UL	UL	15,500	9,500	14,000	9,500	15,000	11,500	6,000
A-4	S	UL	11	3	2	3	2	3	2	1
	A	UL	UL	15,500	9,500	14,000	9,500	15,000	11,500	6,000
A-5	S	UL	UL	UL	UL	UL	UL	UL	UL	UL
	A	UL	UL	UL	UL	UL	UL	UL	UL	UL
B	S	UL	11	5	4	5	4	5	3	2
	A	UL	UL	37,500	23,000	28,500	19,000	36,000	18,000	9,000
E	S	UL	5	3	2	3	2	3	1	1
	A	UL	UL	26,500	14,500	23,500	14,500	25,500	18,500	9,500
F-1	S	UL	11	4	2	3	2	4	2	1
	A	UL	UL	25,000	15,500	19,000	12,000	33,500	14,000	8,500
F-2	S	UL	11	5	3	4	3	5	3	2
	A	UL	UL	37,500	23,000	28,500	18,000	50,500	21,000	13,000
H-1	S	1	1	1	1	1	1	1	1	NP
	A	21,000	16,500	11,000	7,000	9,500	7,000	10,500	7,500	NP
H-2	S	UL	3	2	1	2	1	2	1	1
	A	21,000	16,500	11,000	7,000	9,500	7,000	10,500	7,500	3,000
H-3	S	UL	6	4	2	4	2	4	2	1
	A	UL	60,000	26,500	14,000	17,500	13,000	25,500	10,000	5,000
H-4	S	UL	7	5	3	5	3	5	3	2
	A	UL	UL	37,500	17,500	28,500	17,500	36,000	18,000	6,500
H-5	S	3	3	3	3	3	3	3	3	2
	A	UL	UL	37,500	23,000	28,500	19,000	36,000	18,000	9,000
I-1	S	UL	9	4	3	4	3	4	3	2
	A	UL	55,000	19,000	10,000	16,500	10,000	18,000	10,500	4,500
I-2	S	UL	4	2	1	1	NP	1	1	NP
	A	UL	UL	15,000	11,000	12,000	NP	12,000	9,500	NP
I-3	S	UL	4	2	1	2	1	2	2	1
	A	UL	UL	15,000	11,000	10,500	7,500	12,000	7,500	5,000
I-4	S	UL	5	3	2	3	2	3	1	1
	A	UL	60,500	26,500	13,000	23,500	13,000	25,500	18,500	9,000
M	S	UL	11	4	4	4	4	4	3	1
	A	UL	UL	21,500	12,500	18,500	12,500	20,500	14,000	9,000
R-1	S	UL	11	4	4	4	4	4	3	2
	A	UL	UL	24,000	16,000	24,000	16,000	20,500	12,000	7,000
R-2[a]	S	UL	11	4	4	4	4	4	3	2
	A	UL	UL	24,000	16,000	24,000	16,000	20,500	12,000	7,000
R-3[a]	S	UL	11	4	4	4	4	4	3	3
	A	UL	UL	UL	UL	UL	UL	UL	UL	UL
R-4	S	UL	11	4	4	4	4	4	3	2
	A	UL	UL	24,000	16,000	24,000	16,000	20,500	12,000	7,000
S-1	S	UL	11	4	3	3	3	4	3	1
	A	UL	48,000	26,000	17,500	26,000	17,500	25,500	14,000	9,000
S-2[b, c]	S	UL	11	5	4	4	4	5	4	2
	A	UL	79,000	39,000	26,000	39,000	26,000	38,500	21,000	13,500
U[c]	S	UL	5	4	2	3	2	4	2	1
	A	UL	35,500	19,000	8,500	14,000	8,500	18,000	9,000	5,500

For SI: 1 foot = 304.8 mm, 1 square foot = 0.0929 m².
UL = Unlimited, NP = Not permitted.
a. As applicable in Section 101.2.
b. For open parking structures, see Section 406.3.
c. For private garages, see Section 406.1.

APPENDIX A.4. Figure 3.4. *International Building Code (IBC)* Table 503, Allowable Height and Building Areas (*International Building Code* 2003. Copyright 2002. Falls Church, Virginia: International Code Council, Inc. Reproduced with permission. All rights reserved.)

TABLE 1018.2
BUILDINGS WITH ONE EXIT

OCCUPANCY	MAXIMUM HEIGHT OF BUILDING ABOVE GRADE PLANE	MAXIMUM OCCUPANTS (OR DWELLING UNITS) PER FLOOR AND TRAVEL DISTANCE
A, B[d], E, F, M, U	1 Story	50 occupants and 75 feet travel distance
H-2, H-3	1 Story	3 occupants and 25 feet travel distance
H-4, H-5, I, R	1 Story	10 occupants and 75 feet travel distance
S[a]	1 Story	30 occupants and 100 feet travel distance
B[b], F, M, S[a]	2 Stories	30 occupants and 75 feet travel distance
R-2	2 Stories[c]	4 dwelling units and 50 feet travel distance

TABLE 1014.1
SPACES WITH ONE MEANS OF EGRESS

OCCUPANCY	MAXIMUM OCCUPANT LOAD
A, B, E, F, M, U	50
H-1, H-2, H-3	3
H-4, H-5, I-1, I-3, I-4, R	10
S	30

For SI: 1 foot = 304.8 mm.

a. For the required number of exits for open parking structures, see Section 1018.1.1.

b. For the required number of exits for air traffic control towers, see Section 412.1.

c. Buildings classified as Group R-2 equipped throughout with an automatic sprinkler system in accordance with Section 903.3.1.1 or 903.3.1.2 and provided with emergency escape and rescue openings in accordance with Section 1025 shall have a maximum height of three stories above grade.

d. Buildings equipped throughout with an automatic sprinkler system in accordance with Section 903.3.1.1 with an occupancy in Group B shall have a maximum travel distance of 100 feet.

APPENDIX A.5. Figure 4.15. *International Building Code (IBC)* Table 1018.2, Buildings with One Exit and Table 1014.1, Spaces With One Means of Egress (*International Building Code* 2003. Copyright 2002. Falls Church, Virginia: International Code Council, Inc. Reproduced with permission. All rights reserved.)

TABLE 1015.1
EXIT ACCESS TRAVEL DISTANCE[a]

OCCUPANCY	WITHOUT SPRINKLER SYSTEM (feet)	WITH SPRINKLER SYSTEM (feet)
A, E, F-1, I-1, M, R, S-1	200	250[b]
B	200	300[c]
F-2, S-2, U	300	400[b]
H-1	Not Permitted	75[c]
H-2	Not Permitted	100[c]
H-3	Not Permitted	150[c]
H-4	Not Permitted	175[c]
H-5	Not Permitted	200[c]
I-2, I-3, I-4	150	200[c]

For SI: 1 foot = 304.8 mm.

a. See the following sections for modifications to exit access travel distance requirements:
   Section 402: For the distance limitation in malls.
   Section 404: For the distance limitation through an atrium space.
   Section 1015.2: For increased limitation in Groups F-1 and S-1.
   Section 1024.7: For increased limitation in assembly seating.
   Section 1024.7: For increased limitation for assembly open-air seating.
   Section 1018.2: For buildings with one exit.
   Chapter 31: For the limitation in temporary structures.
b. Buildings equipped throughout with an automatic sprinkler system in accordance with Section 903.3.1.1 or 903.3.1.2. See Section 903 for occupancies where sprinkler systems according to Section 903.3.1.2 are permitted.
c. Buildings equipped throughout with an automatic sprinkler system in accordance with Section 903.3.1.1.

APPENDIX A.6. Figure 4.22. *International Building Code (IBC)* Table 1015.1, Exit Access Travel Distance (*International Building Code* 2003. Copyright 2002. Falls Church, Virginia: International Code Council, Inc. Reproduced with permission. All rights reserved.)

TABLE 1005.1
EGRESS WIDTH PER OCCUPANT SERVED

OCCUPANCY	WITHOUT SPRINKLER SYSTEM		WITH SPRINKLER SYSTEM[a]	
	Stairways (inches per occupant)	Other egress components (inches per occupant)	Stairways (inches per occupant)	Other egress components (inches per occupant)
Occupancies other than those listed below	0.3	0.2	0.2	0.15
Hazardous: H-1, H-2, H-3 and H-4	0.7	0.4	0.3	0.2
Institutional: I-2	NA	NA	0.3	0.2

For SI: 1 inch = 25.4 mm. NA = Not applicable.

a. Buildings equipped throughout with an automatic sprinkler system in accordance with Section 903.3.1.1 or 903.3.1.2.

APPENDIX A.7. Figure 4.17. *International Building Code (IBC)* Table 1005.1, Egress Width per Occupant Served (*International Building Code* 2003. Copyright 2002. Falls Church, Virginia: International Code Council, Inc. Reproduced with permission. All rights reserved.)

TABLE 302.3.2

REQUIRED SEPARATION OF OCCUPANCIES (HOURS)[a]

USE	A-1	A-2	A-3	A-4	A-5	B[b]	E	F-1	F-2	H-1	H-2	H-3	H-4	H-5	I-1	I-2	I-3	I-4	M[b]	R-1	R-2	R-3, R-4	S-1	S-2[c]	U
A-1	—	2	2	2	2	2	2	3	2	NP	4	3	2	4	2	2	2	2	2	2	2	2	3	2	1
A-2[e]		—	2	2	2	2	2	3	2	NP	4	3	2	4	2	2	2	2	2	2	2	2	3	2	1
A-3			—	2	2	2	2	3	2	NP	4	3	2	4	2	2	2	2	2	2	2	2	3	2	1
A-4				—	2	2	2	3	2	NP	4	3	2	4	2	2	2	2	2	2	2	2	3	2	1
A-5					—	2	2	3	2	NP	4	3	2	4	2	2	2	2	2	2	2	2	3	2	1
B[b]						—	2	3	2	NP	2	1	1	1	2	2	2	2	2	2	2	2	3	2	1
E							—	3	2	NP	4	3	1	3	2	2	2	2	2	2	2	2	3	2	1
F-1								—	3	NP	2	1	1	1	4	2	2	2	2	2	4	4	2	2	3
F-2									—	NP	2	1	1	1	2	2	2	2	2	2	3	3	2	1	NP
H-1										—	NP	NP	NP	NP	NP	NP	NP	NP	NP	NP	NP	NP	NP	NP	NP
H-2											—	1	2	2	4	4	4	4	2	4	4	4	2	2	1
H-3												—	1	1	4	3	3	3	1	3	3	3	1	1	3
H-4													—	1	4	4	4	4	1	4	4	4	1	1	2
H-5														—	4	4	3	3	1	4	4	4	1	1	1
I-1															—	2	2	2	2	2	2	2	4	3	3
I-2																—	2	2	2	2	2	2	4	2	2
I-3																	—	2	2	2	2	2	3	2	1
I-4																		—	2	2	2	2	3	2	1
M[b]																			—	2	2	2	3	2	1
R-1																				—	2	2	3	2	1
R-2																					—	2	3	2	1
R-3, R-4																						—	3	2	2
S-1																							—	2[d]	1[d]
S-2[c]																								—	3
U																									—

For SI: 1 square foot = 0.0929 m^2.

NP = Not permitted.

a. See Exception 1 to Section 302.3.2 for reductions permitted.

b. Occupancy separation need not be provided for storage areas within Groups B and M if the:
1. Area is less than 10 percent of the floor area;
2. Area is provided with an automatic fire-extinguishing system and is less than 3,000 square feet; or
3. Area is less than 1,000 square feet.

c. See exception to Section 302.3.2.

d. Areas used only for private or pleasure vehicles shall be allowed to reduce separation by 1 hour.

e. Commercial kitchens need not be separated from the restaurant seating areas that they serve.

APPENDIX A.8. Figure 5.6. *International Building Code (IBC)* Table 302.3.2, Required Separation of Occupancies (Hours) (*International Building Code* 2003. Copyright 2002. Falls Church, Virginia: International Code Council, Inc. Reproduced with permission. All rights reserved.)

TABLE 302.1.1
INCIDENTAL USE AREAS

ROOM OR AREA	SEPARATION[a]
Furnace room where any piece of equipment is over 400,000 Btu per hour input	1 hour or provide automatic fire-extinguishing system
Rooms with any boiler over 15 psi and 10 horsepower	1 hour or provide automatic fire-extinguishing system
Refrigerant machinery rooms	1 hour or provide automatic sprinkler system
Parking garage (Section 406.2)	2 hours; or 1 hour and provide automatic fire-extinguishing system
Hydrogen cut-off rooms	1-hour fire barriers and floor/ceiling assemblies in Group B, F, H, M, S and U occupancies. 2-hour fire barriers and floor/ceiling assemblies in Group A, E, I and R occupancies.
Incinerator rooms	2 hours and automatic sprinkler system
Paint shops, not classified as Group H, located in occupancies other than Group F	2 hours; or 1 hour and provide automatic fire-extinguishing system
Laboratories and vocational shops, not classified as Group H, located in Group E or I-2 occupancies	1 hour or provide automatic fire-extinguishing system
Laundry rooms over 100 square feet	1 hour or provide automatic fire-extinguishing system
Storage rooms over 100 square feet	1 hour or provide automatic fire-extinguishing system
Group I-3 cells equipped with padded surfaces	1 hour
Group I-2 waste and linen collection rooms	1 hour
Waste and linen collection rooms over 100 square feet	1 hour or provide automatic fire-extinguishing system
Stationary lead-acid battery systems having a liquid capacity of more than 100 gallons used for facility standby power, emergency power or uninterrupted power supplies	1-hour fire barriers and floor/ceiling assemblies in Group B, F, H, M, S and U occupancies. 2-hour fire barriers and floor/ceiling assemblies in Group A, E, I and R occupancies

For SI: 1 square foot = 0.0929 m², 1 pound per square inch = 6.9 kPa,
1 British thermal unit = 0.293 watts, 1 horsepower = 746 watts,
1 gallon = 3.785 L.

a. Where an automatic fire-extinguishing system is provided, it need only be provided in the incidental use room or area.

APPENDIX A.9. Figure 5.8. *International Building Code (IBC)* Table 302.1.1, Incidental Use Areas (*International Building Code* 2003. Copyright 2002. Falls Church, Virginia: International Code Council, Inc. Reproduced with permission. All rights reserved.)

TABLE 1016.1
CORRIDOR FIRE-RESISTANCE RATING

OCCUPANCY	OCCUPANT LOAD SERVED BY CORRIDOR	REQUIRED FIRE-RESISTANCE RATING (hours)	
		Without sprinkler system	With sprinkler system[c]
H-1, H-2, H-3	All	Not Permitted	1
H-4, H-5	Greater than 30	Not Permitted	1
A, B, E, F, M, S, U	Greater than 30	1	0
R	Greater than 10	1	0.5
I-2[a], I-4	All	Not Permitted	0
I-1, I-3	All	Not Permitted	1[b]

a. For requirements for occupancies in Group I-2, see Section 407.3.
b. For a reduction in the fire-resistance rating for occupancies in Group I-3, see Section 408.7.
c. Buildings equipped throughout with an automatic sprinkler system in accordance with Section 903.3.1.1 or 903.3.1.2 where allowed.

APPENDIX A.10. Figure 5.11. *International Building Code (IBC)* Table 1016.1, Corridor Fire-Resistance Rating (*International Building Code* 2003. Copyright 2002. Falls Church, Virginia: International Code Council, Inc. Reproduced with permission. All rights reserved.)

TABLE 715.3
FIRE DOOR AND FIRE SHUTTER FIRE PROTECTION RATINGS

TYPE OF ASSEMBLY	REQUIRED ASSEMBLY RATING (hours)	MINIMUM FIRE DOOR AND FIRE SHUTTER ASSEMBLY RATING (hours)
Fire walls and fire barriers having a required fire-resistance rating greater than 1 hour	4	3
	3	3[a]
	2	$1^1/_2$
	$1^1/_2$	$1^1/_2$
Fire barriers having a required fire-resistance rating of 1 hour:		
Shaft exit enclosure and exit passageway walls	1	1
Other fire barriers	1	$^3/_4$
Fire partitions:		
Corridor walls	1	$^1/_3$[b]
	0.5	$^1/_3$[b]
Other fire partitions	1	$^3/_4$
Exterior walls	3	$1^1/_2$
	2	$1^1/_2$
	1	$^3/_4$

a. Two doors, each with a fire protection rating of $1^1/_2$ hours, installed on opposite sides of the same opening in a fire wall, shall be deemed equivalent in fire protection rating to one 3-hour fire door.
b. For testing requirements, see Section 715.3.3.

TABLE 715.4
FIRE WINDOW ASSEMBLY FIRE PROTECTION RATINGS

TYPE OF ASSEMBLY	REQUIRED ASSEMBLY RATING (hours)	MINIMUM FIRE WINDOW ASSEMBLY RATING (hours)
Interior walls:		
Fire walls	All	NP[a]
Fire barriers and fire partitions	> 1	NP[a]
	1	$^3/_4$
Smoke barriers	1	$^3/_4$
Exterior walls	>1	$1^1/_2$
	1	$^3/_4$
Party walls	All	NP[a]

a. Not permitted except as specified in Section 715.2.

APPENDIX A.11. Figure 5.12. *International Building Code (IBC)* Table 715.3, Fire Door and Fire Shutter Fire Protection Ratings and Table 715.4, Fire Window Assembly Fire Protection Ratings (*International Building Code* 2003. Copyright 2002. Falls Church, Virginia: International Code Council, Inc. Reproduced with permission. All rights reserved.)

TABLE 716.3.1
FIRE DAMPER RATING

TYPE OF PENETRATION	MINIMUM DAMPER RATING (hour)
Less than 3-hour fire-resistance-rated assemblies	1.5
3-hour or greater fire-resistance-rated assemblies	3

APPENDIX A.12. Figure 5.16. *International Building Code (IBC)* Table 716.3.1, Fire Damper Rating (*International Building Code* 2003. Copyright 2002. Falls Church, Virginia: International Code Council, Inc. Reproduced with permission. All rights reserved.)

TABLE 403.1
MINIMUM NUMBER OF REQUIRED PLUMBING FIXTURES
(See Sections 403.2 and 403.3)

NO.	CLASSIFICATION	USE GROUP	DESCRIPTION	WATER CLOSETS (URINALS SEE SECTION 419.2) MALE	FEMALE	LAVATORIES MALE	FEMALE	BATHTUBS/ SHOWERS	DRINKING FOUNTAIN (SEE SECTION 410.1)	OTHER
1	Assembly (see Sections 403.2, 403.5 and 403.6)	A-1	Theaters usually with fixed seats and other buildings for the performing arts and motion pictures	1 per 125	1 per 65	1 per 200		—	1 per 500	1 service sink
		A-2	Nightclubs, bars, taverns, dance halls and buildings for similar purposes	1 per 40	1 per 40	1 per 75		—	1 per 500	1 service sink
			Restaurants, banquet halls and food courts	1 per 75	1 per 75	1 per 200		—	1 per 500	1 service sink
		A-3	Auditoriums without permanent seating, art galleries, exhibition halls, museums, lecture halls, libraries, arcades and gymnasiums	1 per 125	1 per 65	1 per 200		—	1 per 500	1 service sink
			Passenger terminals and transportation facilities	1 per 500	1 per 500	1 per 750		—	1 per 1,000	1 service sink
			Places of worship and other religious services. Churches without assembly halls	1 per 150	1 per 75	1 per 200		—	1 per 1,000	1 service sink
		A-4	Coliseums, arenas, skating rinks, pools and tennis courts for indoor sporting events and activities	1 per 75 for the first 1,500 and 1 per 120 for the remainder exceeding 1,500	1 per 40 for the first 1,500 and 1 per 60 for the remainer exceeding 1,500	1 per 200	1 per 150	—	1 per 1,000	1 service sink
		A-5	Stadiums, amusement parks, bleachers and grandstands for outdoor sporting events and activities	1 per 75 for the first 1,500 and 1 per 120 for the remainder exceeding 1,500	1 per 40 for the first 1,500 and 1 per 60 for the remainder exceeding 1,500	1 per 200	1 per 150	—	1 per 1,000	1 service sink
2	Business (see Sections 403.2, 403.4 and 403.6)	B	Buildings for the transaction of business, professional services, other services involving merchandise, office buildings, banks, light industrial and similar uses	1 per 25 for the first 50 and 1 per 50 for the remainder exceeding 50		1 per 40 for the first 50 and 1 per 80 for the remainder exceeding 50		—	1 per 100	1 service sink
3	Educational	E	Educational facilities	1 per 50		1 per 50		—	1 per 100	1 service sink
4	Factory and industrial	F-1 and F-2	Structures in which occupants are engaged in work fabricating, assembly or processing of products or materials	1 per 100		1 per 100		(see Section 411)	1 per 400	1 service sink

APPENDIX A.13. Figure 7.1. *International Plumbing Code® (IPC®)* Table 403.1, Minimum Number of Required Plumbing Fixtures (*International Plumbing Code* 2003. Copyright 2003. Falls Church, Virginia: International Code Council, Inc. Reproduced with permission. All rights reserved.)

(continued on the following page)

NO.	CLASSIFICATION	USE GROUP	DESCRIPTION	WATER CLOSETS (URINALS SEE SECTION 419.2) MALE	WATER CLOSETS (URINALS SEE SECTION 419.2) FEMALE	LAVATORIES MALE	LAVATORIES FEMALE	BATHTUBS/ SHOWERS	DRINKING FOUNTAIN (SEE SECTION 410.1)	OTHER
5	Institutional	I-1	Residential care	1 per 10		1 per 10		1 per 8	1 per 100	1 service sink
		I-2	Hospitals, ambulatory nursing home patients [b]	1 per room [c]		1 per room [c]		1 per 15	1 per 100	1 service sink per floor
			Employees, other than residential care [b]	1 per 25		1 per 35		—	1 per 100	—
			Visitors, other than residential care	1 per 75		1 per 100		—	1 per 500	—
		I-3	Prisons [b]	1 per cell		1 per cell		1 per 15	1 per 100	1 service sink
		I-3	Reformitories, detention centers, and correctional centers [b]	1 per 15		1 per 15		1 per 15	1 per 100	1 service sink
		I-4	Adult daycare and childcare [b]	1 per 15		1 per 15		1 per 15 [d]	1 per 100	1 service sink
6	Mercantile (see Sections 403.2, 403.5 and 403.6)	M	Retail stores, service stations, shops, salesrooms, markets and shopping centers	1 per 500		1 per 750		—	1 per 1,000	1 service sink
7	Residential	R-1	Hotels, motels, boarding houses (transient)	1 per guestroom		1 per guestroom		1 per guestroom	—	1 service sink
		R-2	Dormitories, fraternities, sororities and boarding houses (not transient)	1 per 10		1 per 10		1 per 8	1 per 100	1 service sink
		R-2	Apartment house	1 per dwelling unit		1 per dwelling unit		1 per dwelling unit	—	1 kitchen sink per dwelling unit; 1 automatic clothes washer connection per 20 dwelling units [e]
		R-3	One- and two-family dwellings	1 per dwelling unit		1 per dwelling unit		1 per dwelling unit	—	1 kitchen sink per dwelling unit; 1 automatic clothes washer connector per dwelling unit [e]
		R-4	Residential care/assisted living facilities	1 per 10		1 per 10		1 per 8	1 per 100	1 service sink
8	Storage (see Sections 403.2 and 403.4)	S-1 S-2	Structures for the storage of goods, warehouses, storehouse and freight depots. Low and Moderate Hazard.	1 per 100		1 per 100		1 per 1,000	See Section 411	1 service sink

a. The fixtures shown are based on one fixture being the minimum required for the number of persons indicated or any fraction of the number of persons indicated. The number of occupants shall be determined by the *International Building Code*.

b. Toilet facilities for employees shall be separate from facilities for inmates or patients.

c. A single-occupant toilet room with one water closet and one lavatory serving not more than two adjacent patient rooms shall be permitted where such room is provided with direct access from each patient room and with provisions for privacy.

d. For day nurseries, a maximum of one bathtub shall be required.

e. For attached one- and two-family dwellings, one automatic clothes washer connection shall be required per 20 dwelling units.

APPENDIX A.13 (*continued*)

Table A.10.2.2 Interior Finish Classification Limitations

Occupancy	Exits	Exit Access Corridors	Other Spaces
Assembly — New			
>300 occupant load	A	A or B	A or B
	I or II	I or II	
≤300 occupant load	A	A or B	A, B, or C
	I or II	I or II	
Assembly — Existing			
>300 occupant load	A	A or B	A or B
≤300 occupant load	A	A or B	A, B, or C
Educational — New	A	A or B	A or B;
	I or II	I or II	C on low partitions[†]
Educational — Existing	A	A or B	A, B, or C
Day-Care Centers — New	A	A	A or B
	I or II	I or II	
Day-Care Centers — Existing	A or B	A or B	A or B
Day-Care Homes — New	A or B	A or B	A, B, or C
	I or II		
Day-Care Homes — Existing	A or B	A, B, or C	A, B, or C
Health Care — New	A	A	A
		B on lower portion of corridor wall[†]	B in small individual rooms[†]
Health Care — Existing	A or B	A or B	A or B
Detention and Correctional — New (sprinklers mandatory)	A or B	A or B	A, B, or C
	I or II	I or II	
Detention and Correctional — Existing	A or B	A or B	A, B, or C
	I or II	I or II	
1- and 2-Family Dwellings, Lodging or Rooming Houses	A, B, or C	A, B, or C	A, B, or C
Hotels and Dormitories — New	A	A or B	A, B, or C
	I or II	I or II	
Hotels and Dormitories — Existing	A or B	A or B	A, B, or C
	I or II[†]	I or II[†]	
Apartment Buildings — New	A	A or B	A, B, or C
	I or II	I or II	
Apartment Buildings — Existing	A or B	A or B	A, B, or C
	I or II[†]	I or II[†]	
Residential, Board and Care — (See Chapter 32 and Chapter 33)			
Mercantile — New	A or B	A or B	A or B
	I or II		
Mercantile — Existing Class A or Class B Stores	A or B	A or B	Ceilings — A or B; walls — A, B, or C
Mercantile — Existing Class C Stores	A, B, or C	A, B, or C	A, B, or C
Business and Ambulatory Health Care — New	A or B	A or B	A, B, or C
	I or II		
Business and Ambulatory Health Care — Existing	A or B	A or B	A, B, or C
Industrial	A or B	A, B, or C	A, B, or C
	I or II	I or II	
Storage	A or B	A, B, or C	A, B, or C
	I or II	I or II	

Notes:
1. Class A interior wall and ceiling finish — flame spread 0–25, (new) smoke developed 0–450.
2. Class B interior wall and ceiling finish — flame spread 26–75, (new) smoke developed 0–450.
3. Class C interior wall and ceiling finish — flame spread 76–200, (new) smoke developed 0–450.
4. Class I interior floor finish — critical radiant flux, not less than 0.45 W/cm².
5. Class II interior floor finish — critical radiant flux, not less than 0.22 W/cm² but less than 0.45 W/cm².
6. Automatic sprinklers — where a complete standard system of automatic sprinklers is installed, interior wall and ceiling finish with flame spread rating not exceeding Class C is permitted to be used in any location where Class B is required and with rating of Class B in any location where Class A is required; similarly, Class II interior floor finish is permitted to be used in any location where Class I is required, and no critical radiant flux rating is required where Class II is required. These provisions do not apply to new detention and correctional occupancies.
7. Exposed portions of structural members complying with the requirements for heavy timber construction are permitted.
†See corresponding chapters for details.

Appendix A.14. Figure 9.14. *Life Safety Code (LSC)* Table A.10.2.2, Interior Finish Classification Limitations (Reprinted with permission from NFPA 101-2003, *Life Safety Code*®, Copyright © 2003, National Fire Protection Association, Quincy, MA 02169. This reprinted material is not the complete and official position of the NFPA on the referenced subject, which is represented only by the standard in its entirety.)

APPENDIX B

FULL-SIZE CHECKLISTS

Each chapter (except Chapter 3) in *The Codes Guidebook for Interiors* has a codes checklist. These same checklists have been reprinted in this appendix. The full-size format will make them easier to use. You may copy them, revise them, and use them for your various design projects.

For an explanation of how to use the checklists, refer to the *Guidebook*. They can be found at the end of each chapter in the *Guidebook*.

Interior Codes and Standards Checklist

Date:_____

Project Name:_____

PUBLICATIONS REQUIRED	YEAR OF EDITION	YEAR OF AMENDMENT (if required)	RESEARCH DATE
Codes and Regulations			
BUILDING CODE - Circle One: IBC NFPA 5000 OTHER _____	_____	_____	__/__/__
Structural Engineer Required? _____ YES _____ NO			
PERFORMANCE CODE - Circle One: ICCPC NFPA[1] OTHER _____	_____	_____	__/__/__
FIRE CODE - Circle One: IFC UFC OTHER _____	_____	_____	__/__/__
LIFE SAFETY CODE (NFPA 101)	_____	_____	__/__/__
PLUMBING CODE - Circle One: IPC UPC OTHER _____	_____	_____	__/__/__
Plumbing Engineer Required? _____ YES _____ NO			
MECHANICAL CODE - Circle One: IMC UMC OTHER _____	_____	_____	__/__/__
Mechanical Engineer Required? _____ YES _____ NO			
ELECTRIC CODE - Circle One: ICCEC NEC OTHER _____	_____	_____	__/__/__
Electrical Engineer Required? _____ YES _____ NO			
ENERGY CODE - Circle One: IECC NFPA 900 OTHER _____	_____	_____	__/__/__
Engineer Required? _____ Structural _____ Electrical _____ Mechanical			
RESIDENTIAL CODE - Circle One: IRC OTHER _____	_____	_____	__/__/__
EXISTING BUILDING CODE - Circle One: IEBC OTHER _____	_____	_____	__/__/__
ACCESSIBILITY REGULATIONS/STANDARDS			
ADA Guidelines[2]	_____	_____	__/__/__
ICC/ANSI A117.1 Accessible and Usable Buildings and Facilities	_____	_____	__/__/__
Other: _____	_____	_____	__/__/__
OTHER: [3] _____	_____	_____	__/__/__
_____	_____	_____	__/__/__
_____	_____	_____	__/__/__
_____	_____	_____	__/__/__
Standards [4]			
NATIONAL FIRE PROTECTION ASSOCIATION (NFPA):			
NFPA ____ _____	_____	_____	__/__/__
NFPA ____ _____	_____	_____	__/__/__
NFPA ____ _____	_____	_____	__/__/__
AMERICAN SOCIETY OF TESTING & MATERIALS (ASTM)			
ASTM ____ _____	_____	_____	__/__/__
ASTM ____ _____	_____	_____	__/__/__
UNDERWRITERS LABORATORIES (UL)			
UL ____ _____	_____	_____	__/__/__
UL ____ _____	_____	_____	__/__/__
OTHER: _____	_____	_____	__/__/__
_____	_____	_____	__/__/__
_____	_____	_____	__/__/__

NOTES:

1. Circle NFPA if you are using another NFPA document and plan to use a performance-based requirement listed in that document.

2. All projects should be reviewed for ADA compatibility with few exceptions (i.e., federal buildings, religious facilities, one/two family homes).

3. Be sure to check for other state and local codes. Local codes can include special ordinances, health codes, zoning regulations, and historic preservation laws. List the specific ones.

4. Refer to the codes as well as local requirements to determine which standards are required. List the specific publications.

APPENDIX B.1. Figure 1.5. Interior Codes and Standards Checklist

Occupancy Checklist

Date:_____

Project Name: _____ Space: _____

Code Source Used (check all that apply): __ IBC __ LSC __ NFPA 5000 __ OTHER: _____

Occupancy Risk Factors/Hazards (check those that apply):

__ High number of occupants	__ Occupant generally unfamiliar with space
__ Occupants resting or sleeping	__ Unusual characteristics of building/space
__ Alertness of occupants	__ Potential for spread of fire
__ Mobility of occupants	__ Hazardous materials stored or used
__ Age of occupants	__ Type of hazard: _____
__ Security measures	__ Other: _____

Occupancy Considerations (check those that apply): [1]

__ Single Occupancy (may require more than one calculation based on types of use and/or load factors)

__ Incidental Use (if separated according to code, include in main occupancy; if not, may need to calculate separately)

__ Accessory Use (occupant load calculated separately from main occupancy; may need to include with main for exiting)

__ Separated - Mixed or Multiple Occupancy (calculate occupant load for each occupancy)

__ Non-Separated Mixed Occupancy (IBC only) (use strictest occupancy requirements)

__ Mixed Multiple Occupancy (NFPA only) (calculate occupant load for each occupancy)

__ Occupancy with Fixed Seats (may need to calculate fixed seats and surrounding open areas)

Occupancy Loads [1]

Calculation 1 - Occupancy Classification: _____

Building Use (__ NEW __EXISTING): _____

__ Load Factor [2] (__ GROSS __NET): _____

__ Fixed Seat Variable (__ WITH ARMS __CONTINUOUS __ BENCH): _____

Actual Floor Area (__ GROSS __NET):_____ OR Number/Length of Fixed Seats: _____

Occupant Load 1 (__ USING LOAD FACTOR FORMULA __ BASED ON FIXED SEATS): _____

Calculation 2 - Occupancy Classification: _____

Building Use (__ NEW __EXISTING): _____

__ Load Factor [2] (__ GROSS __NET): _____

__ Fixed Seat Variable (__ WITH ARMS __CONTINUOUS __ BENCH): _____

Actual Floor Area (__ GROSS __NET):_____ OR Number/Length of Fixed Seats: _____

Occupant Load 2 (__ USING LOAD FACTOR FORMULA __ BASED ON FIXED SEATS): _____

Calculation 3 - Occupancy Classification: _____

Building Use (__ NEW __EXISTING): _____

__ Load Factor [2] (__ GROSS __NET): _____

__ Fixed Seat Variable (__ WITH ARMS __CONTINUOUS __ BENCH): _____

Actual Floor Area (__ GROSS __NET):_____ OR Number/Length of Fixed Seats: _____

Occupant Load 3 (__ USING LOAD FACTOR FORMULA __ BASED ON FIXED SEATS): _____

Total Calculated Occupant Load: _____ (__ SPACE __FLOOR __ BUILDING)

Adjusted Occupant Load - Based on Actual Needs: _____

Local Code Approval (when required)

__ NO __YES NAME: _____ DATE: _____

NOTES:

1. If there is more than one main occupancy in the same space or building, you may want to use a separate checklist for each.

2. If you are using a gross load factor you may need to include shared common spaces in addition to the ancillary spaces.

APPENDIX B.2. Figure 2.13. Occupancy Checklist

Means of Egress Checklist

Date:_____

Project Name:_____ Space: _____

Main Occupancy (new or existing):_____ Occupant Load: _____

Type of Space (check one): _____ Building _____ Floor _____ Space/Tenant _____ Room

---

Exit Access Requirements (if more than 2 attach additional calculations)

   Exit Access 1 (check/research those that apply and fill in the corresponding information)

   Type of Component(s): __ DOOR __STAIR __ RAMP __CORRIDOR __ AISLE __ INTERVENING ROOMS

   Required Width: _____ Using: __ LEVEL VARIABLE __STAIR VARIABLE __OTHER VARIABLE

   Exit Access 2 (check/research those that apply and fill in the corresponding information)

   Type of Component(s): __ DOOR __STAIR __ RAMP __CORRIDOR __ AISLE __ INTERVENING ROOMS

   Required Width: _____ Using: __ LEVEL VARIABLE __STAIR VARIABLE __OTHER VARIABLE

Travel Distance (check those that apply and indicate lengths where required)

   __ Common Path of Travel: _____ __ Max. allowed travel distance for space: _____

   __ Dead-End Corridor: _____ __ Max. allowed travel distance for floor/building: _____

Exit Requirements (may require up to 4 exits, if more than 2 attach additional calculations)

   Required Number of Exits (check those that apply and indicate quantity where shown)

   __ One Exit Exception   __ Required Number of Exits: _____

   __ Minimum of Two Exits   __ Number of Exits Provided: _____

Location of Exits Determined By (check one)

   __ 1/2 Diagonal Rule   __ Other Remoteness Requirement

   __ 1/3 Diagonal Rule   Explain: _____

Exit 1 (Check/research those that apply and fill in the corresponding information)

   Type: __ EXTERIOR DOOR __EXIT STAIR __ EXIT PASSAGEWAY __HORIZONTAL EXIT __ AREA OF REFUGE

   Required Width: _____ Using: __ LEVEL VARIABLE __STAIR VARIABLE __MINIMUM REQUIRED

   Number of Doors: _____ Distributed: __ EVENLY AMONG EXITS __ASSEMBLY EXCEPTION

   Exit 2 (Check/research those that apply and fill in the corresponding information)

   Type: __ EXTERIOR DOOR __EXIT STAIR __ EXIT PASSAGEWAY __HORIZONTAL EXIT __ AREA OF REFUGE

   Required Width: _____ Using: __ LEVEL VARIABLE __STAIR VARIABLE __MINIMUM REQUIRED

   Number of Doors: _____ Distributed: __ EVENLY AMONG EXITS __ASSEMBLY EXCEPTION

Exit Discharge Components (check those that apply and research if required)

   __ MAIN LOBBY __ FOYER __VESTIBULE(S) __DISCHARGE CORRIDOR(S) __EXIT COURT(S)

Other Code and Accessibility Requirements to Consider (check/research those that apply)

   __ Doors: Type, Swing, Size, Hardware, Threshold, Clearances, Fire Rating

   __ Stairs: Type, Riser Height, Tread Depth, Nosing, Width, Handrail, Guard, Fire Rating

   __ Ramps: Slope, Rise, Landings, Width, Edge Detail, Finish, Handrail, Guard

   __ Corridors: Length, Width, Protruding Objects, Fire Rating

   __ Aisles: Fixed Seats, No Fixed Seats, Ramp(s), Steps, Handrails

   __ Intervening Rooms: Type, Size, Obstructions, Fire Rating

NOTES:

1. Refer to codes and standards for specific information as well as ADA guidelines and ICC/ANSI standards for additional requirements.

2. Attach any floor plans indicating locations of components and other paperwork required for calculations.

3. Check specific occupancy classifications and/or building types for special requirements that may apply.

APPENDIX B.3. Figure 4.26. Means of Egress Checklist

Fire Resistance Checklist

Date:_____

Project Name:_____ Space: _____

Occupancy (new or existing):_____

Type of Construction: _____

REQUIRED FIRE PROTECTION (check those that apply)	EXT'G (yes/no)	LOCATION IN BUILDING	TYPE OF MATERIAL OR ASSEMBLY REQUIRED (list information)	HOURLY RATING OR FIRE TEST REQUIRED (list type)

Fire Barriers and Partitions [1]
 __ Fire Wall(s)
 __ Fire Area(s)
 __ Occupancy Separation(s)
 __ Tenant Separation(s)
 __ Incidental Use Area/Room(s)
 __ Vertical Shaft Enclosure(s)
 __ Means of Egress Component(s)
    __ Exit Stairway(s)
    __ Exit Access Stairway(s)
    __ Horizontal Exit(s)
    __ Exit Corridor/Passageway(s)
    __ Exit Access Corridor(s)
 __ Floor/Ceiling Assembly(ies)
 __ Other:_____				

Smoke Barriers and Partitions [1] __ Smoke Compartment(s) __ Vertical Shaft(s) __ Vestibule(s) __ Other:_____				

Opening Protectives
 __ Rated Door Assembly(ies)
    __ Fire Door(s)
    __ Smoke Door(s)
 __ Fire Window Assembly(ies)
 __ Rated Glazing and Frame(s)
 __ Special Hardware
 __ Other:_____				

Through-Penetration Protectives
 Engineer Required? ___YES ___ NO
 __ Firestop(s)
 __ Fireblock(s)
 __ Draftstop(s)
 __ Damper System(s)
    __ Fire Damper(s)
    __ Smoke Damper(s)
 __ Other:_____				

NOTES:

1 Remember that fire and smoke barriers need to be considered both vertically and horizontally.

2. Refer to codes and standards for specific information. Also check the ADA guidelines and ICC/ANSI standard for accessibility-related requirement

3. Attach all testing verification, including copies of manufacturer labels and/or copies of rated assembly details.

APPENDIX B.4. Figure 5.20. Fire-Resistance Checklist

Fire Protection Checklist

Date:_____

Project Name:_____ Space: _____

Occupancy (new or existing):_____

Type of Construction:_____

REQUIRED FIRE PROTECTION (check those that apply)	EXT'G (yes/no)	LOCATION(S) IN BUILDING	TYPE OF SYSTEM/ ITEM REQUIRED (list information)	QUANTITIES REQUIRED (new or add'l)
Detection Systems Engineer Required? ___YES ___ NO __ Smoke Detector(s) __ Heat Detector(s) __ Manual Fire Alarm(s) __ Other:_____				
Alarm Systems Engineer Required? ___YES ___ NO __ Visual/Audible Alarm(s) __ Audible only __ Visual only __ Voice Communication System(s) __ Accessible Warning System(s) __ Emergency Alarm(s) __ Other:_____				
Extinguishing Systems Engineer Required? ___YES ___ NO __ Fire Extinguisher(s) __ Fire Extinguisher Cabinet(s) __ Standpipe(s) __ Fire Hose(s) __ Sprinkler System(s) __ Types of Head(s) __ Orientation of Head(s) __ Alternate System(s) __ Other:_____				

NOTES:

1. Refer to codes and standards for specific information as well as ADA guidelines and ICC/ANSI standard for additional requirements.
2. If automatic sprinkler systems are used, make sure they are approved and check for possible code trade-offs.
3. Consult and coordinate detection/alarm systems with electrical engineers and extinguishing systems with mechanical engineers.
4. Be sure to note on floor plans the location of fire-rated walls and floor/ceilings for placement of required fire dampers and fire stops.

APPENDIX B.5. Figure 6.7. Fire Protection Checklist

Plumbing and Mechanical Checklist

Date:_____

Project Name:_____ Space: _____

Occupancy (new or existing):_____Occupant Load: _____

Building Type:_____

Plumbing Requirements [2]   Engineer Required? ___ YES ___ NO

Type and Quantity of Plumbing Fixtures (check those that apply and insert quantities)

Fixture	TOTAL FIXTURES Required	ACCESSIBLE FIXTURES New	Existing	STANDARD FIXTURES New	Existing
__ Water Closet	M___/F ___	M___/F ___	M___/F ___	M___/F ___	M___/F ___
__ Urinal	M___/F ___	M___/F ___	M___/F ___	M___/F ___	M___/F ___
__ Lavatory	M___/F ___	M___/F ___	M___/F ___	M___/F ___	M___/F ___
__ Sink	M___/F ___	M___/F ___	M___/F ___	M___/F ___	M___/F ___
__ Drinking Fountain	M___/F ___	M___/F ___	M___/F ___	M___/F ___	M___/F ___
__ Bathtub	M___/F ___	M___/F ___	M___/F ___	M___/F ___	M___/F ___
__ Shower	M___/F ___	M___/F ___	M___/F ___	M___/F ___	M___/F ___
__ Other _____	M___/F ___	M___/F ___	M___/F ___	M___/F ___	M___/F ___
__ Other _____	M___/F ___	M___/F ___	M___/F ___	M___/F ___	M___/F ___

Type of Facility Required (check those that apply)

Toilet Facilities: ___ Single (Separate M/F)   ___ Single (Shared Unisex)   ___ Single (Family Style)
___ Multi-Toilet: quantity (if more than one each M/F) _____

Bathing Facilities: ___ Single (Separate M/F) ___Single (Shared Unisex) ___Single (Family Style)
___ Multi-Toilet: quantity (if more than one each M/F) _____

Other Plumbing Code and Accessibility Requirements to Consider (Check/research those that apply)

__ Fixtures: Mounting Heights, Clear Floor Space, Faucet/Control Location, Projections, Water Consumption
__ Faucet/Controls: Ease of Operation (i.e., lever, automatic, etc.), Water Consumption, Water Temperature
__ Grab Bars: Location, Lengths, Heights, Orientation, Additional for Special Situation
__ Accessories: Mounting Heights, Control Locations, Projections, Clear Floor Space
__ Finishes: Smooth/Nonabsorbent, Slip Resistant, Thresholds, Special Locations
__ Room: Turning Space, Overlapping Clear Floor Space, Privacy, Signage, Stall Size, Door Swing

Mechanical Requirements [2]   Engineer Required? ___ YES ___ NO

Type of Mechanical System: _____

Location of Mechanical Room: _____Size: _____

Type of Air Circulation (Duct or Plenum): _____

Ventilation Required (Type and Locations): _____

Exhaust System Required (Type and Location): _____

Ceiling Heights Required (Minimums and Clearances): _____

Location and Type of Supply Diffusers (Ceiling, Wall, Floor): _____

Location and Type of Return Grills (Ceiling, Wall, Floor): _____

Number and Location of Thermostats/Zones: _____

NOTES:
1. Refer to codes and standards for specific information. Also check the ADA guidelines and ICC/ANSI standard for accessible mounting locations.
2. See Chapter 6 checklist for additional plumbing and mechanical related requirements such as automatic sprinkler systems, dampers, etc.
3. Be sure to note on floor plans the location of fire-rated walls/ceilings for placement of required supply diffusers and return grills.

APPENDIX B.6. Figure 7.13. Plumbing and Mechanical Checklist

Electrical and Communication Checklist

Date:_____

Project Name:_____ Space: _____

Occupancy (new or existing):_____

Electrical Requirements   Engineer Required?   ___ YES   ___ NO

Types of Electrical Panels (check those that apply and note locations, sizes, etc.)

__ Switchboard: _____

__ Panel Board(s): _____

__ Branch Panel Board(s): _____

Special Cabling Conditions : _____   Conduit Required: __YES __NO

Location of Receptacle Outlets : _____

__ EXISTING   __ NEW (Rating of wall(s): _____)

Location of Switches : _____

__ EXISTING   __ NEW (Rating of wall(s): _____)

Special Types of Outlets and/or Circuits (check those that apply and note locations)

__ Dedicated Outlets: _____

__ Ground Fault Circuit Interrupters (GFCI): _____

__ Arc Fault Circuit Interrupters (AFCI): _____

__ Other: _____

Types of Required Equipment (check those that apply, list new and existing, specify if over 120V)

__ Light Fixtures: _____

__ Appliances: _____

__ Equipment: _____

Types of Electrical Systems (check those that apply, list new and existing, etc.)

__ Emergency Electrical System: _____

__ Required Standby System: _____

__ Optional Standby System: _____

__ Uninterrupted Power Supply System (UPS): _____

Communication Requirements   Engineer Required?   ___ YES   ___ NO

Type of Communication Systems [3]   (check those that apply and insert information)

SYSTEM	VENDOR OR CONSULTANT	CENTRAL LOCATION OF SYSTEM	TYPE OF CABLING OR SPECIAL NOTES
___ Building Telephone System	_____	_____	_____
___ Public Telephone System	_____	_____	_____
___ Computer System	_____	_____	_____
___ Cable TV Services	_____	_____	_____
___ Closed Circuit TV System	_____	_____	_____
___ Satellite TV System	_____	_____	_____
___ Voice Notification System	_____	_____	_____
___ Intercom System	_____	_____	_____
___ Assistive Listening System	_____	_____	_____
___ Audio/Visual System	_____	_____	_____
___ Security System	_____	_____	_____
___ Other _____	_____	_____	_____

NOTES:

1. Refer to codes and standards for specifics. Also check the ADA guideline and ICC/ANSI standard for accessible mounting locations.

2. Be sure to note on floor plans the location of fire-rated walls for placement of required fire dampers and fire stops.

3. Also see checklist in Chapter 6 for information on various alarm and other notification type systems as required by the codes.

APPENDIX B.7. Figure 8.10. Electrical and Communication Checklist

Finishes and Furniture Checklist

Date:_____

Project Name:_____ Space: _____

Occupancy (new or existing):_____

Type of Space (check one): _____ Exit _____ Exit Access _____ Other Space

REGULATED FINISHES AND FURNISHINGS (check those that apply)	TEST METHOD REQUIRED (fill in test name)	MANUFACTURER AND CATALOG #	MANUFACTURER TESTED (yes or no)	FINISH TREATMENT (yes or no)	DATE COMPLETED
Wallcoverings __ Vinyl Wallcovering __ Textile Wallcovering __ Expanded Vinyl Wallcovering __ Carpet Wallcovering __ Light-Transmitting Plastics __ Wood Paneling __ Wood Veneers __ Decorative Molding/Trim __ Other:_____					
Ceiling Finishes __ Ceiling Tile __ Textile Ceiling Finish __ Plastic Light Diffusing Panels __ Decorative Ceiling __ Decorative Molding/Trim __ Other:_____					
Floor Coverings __ Carpet (Broadloom) __ Carpet Tile __ Rugs __ Carpet Padding __ Resilient Flooring __ Hardwood Flooring __ Other:_____					
Window Treatments __ Draperies __ Liners __ Blinds __ Wood Shutters __ Other:_____					
Furnishings/Furniture __ Fabric __ Vinyl/Leather __ Batting __ Welt Cord __ Interliners __ Filling __ Seating __ Mattresses __ Plastic Laminates/Veneers __ Other:_____					

NOTES:

1. Refer to codes and standards for specific information. Also check the ADA guidelines and ICC/ANSI standard for accessibility related finish and furniture requirements.

2. Attach all testing verification including copies of manufacturer labels and treatment certificates.

APPENDIX B.8. Figure 9.21. Finishes and Furniture Checklist

Summary Interior Project Checklist

Date:_____

Project Name:_____ Space: _____

1 DETERMINE WHICH CODES ARE REQUIRED (Chapter 1)
___ Building Code
___ Fire Code
___ Performance Code
___ Other Code Publications
___ Local Codes and Ordinances
___ Government Regulations
___ Standards and Tests

2 OCCUPANCY REQUIREMENTS (Chapter 2)
___ Determine Building Types(s)
___ Determine Occupancy Classification(s)
___ Calculate Occupant Load(s)
___ Adjustments to Occupant Load(s)
___ Review Specific Occupancy Requirements
___ Compare Code and Accessibility Requirements

3 MINIMUM TYPES OF CONSTRUCTION (Chapter 3)
___ Determine Construction Type
___ Determine Ratings of Building Elements
___ Calculate Maximum Floor Area (as required)
___ Calculate Building Height (as required)
___ Review Construction Type Limitations

4 MEANS OF EGRESS REQUIREMENTS (Chapter 4)
___ Determine Quantity and Types of Means of Egress
___ Calculate Minimum Widths
___ Determine Arrangement of Exits
___ Calculate Travel Distance
___ Determine Required Signage
___ Compare Code and Accessibility Requirements
___ Review Emergency Light Requirements

5 FIRE RESISTANCE REQUIREMENTS (Chapter 5)
___ Determine Use of Fire Walls
___ Determine Fire Barriers and Partitions
___ Determine Smoke Barriers and Partitions
___ Determine Location of Opening Protectives
___ Determine Location of Through Penetration Protectives
___ Review Types of Fire Tests and Ratings Required
___ Compare Code and Standard Requirements
___ Review Requirements During Assembly Specification
___ Check All Enforced Standards

6 FIRE PROTECTION REQUIREMENTS (Chapter 6)
___ Determine Fire and Smoke Detection Systems
___ Determine Required Alarm Systems
___ Determine Types of Extinguishing Systems
___ Review for Possible Sprinkler Tradeoffs
___ Compare Code and Accessibility Requirements
___ Coordinate with Engineer (as required)

7 PLUMBING REQUIREMENTS (Chapter 7)
___ Determine Types of Fixtures Required
___ Calculate Number of Each Fixture Required
___ Determine Required Toilet/Bathing Facilities
___ Review for Finishes, Accessories and Signage
___ Compare Code and Accessibility Requirements
___ Coordinate with Engineer (as required)

8 MECHANICAL REQUIREMENTS (Chapter 7)
___ Determine Type of Air Distribution System(s)
___ Determine Items Affecting Cooling Loads
___ Determine Access and Clearance Requirements
___ Figure Zoning and Thermostat Locations
___ Check for Accessibility and Energy Efficiency Compliance
___ Coordinate with Engineer (as required)

9 ELECTRICAL REQUIREMENTS (Chapter 8)
___ Determine Types/Locations of Outlets, Switches, Fixtures
___ Determine Emergency Power and Lighting Requirements
___ Check for Accessibility and Energy Efficiency Compliance
___ Compare Requirements During Selection/Specification
___ Coordinate with Engineer (as required)

10 COMMUNICATION REQUIREMENTS (Chapter 8)
___ Determine Systems Required by Client
___ Compare Needs versus Code/Standard Requirements
___ Check for Accessibility Compliance
___ Coordinate with Engineer/Consultant (as required)

11 FINISH AND FURNITURE REQUIREMENTS (Chapter 9)
___ Review Tests and Types of Ratings Required
___ Determine Special Finish Requirements
___ Determine Special Furniture Requirements
___ Compare Code and Accessibility Requirements
___ Compare Requirements During Selection/Specification
___ Check All Enforced Standards

NOTE: Be sure to review all codes and standards required in the jurisdiction as well as required federal regulations. Consult the jurisdiction having authority at any step in question.

APPENDIX B.9. Figure 10.4. Summary Interior Project Checklist